George Meikle Kemp

George Meikle Kemp

Architect of the Scott Monument

by
Morven Leese

Morven Leese

Cover portraits

Front: *George Meikle Kemp* (modelled by Alexander Handyside Ritchie, carved in marble by John Hutchison).

Back: *George Meikle Kemp (1795-1844), with the Model for the Scott Monument, Edinburgh* (by an unknown artist). Unveiled at the Scott Monument on 3 March 2011 by Remy Fourmoy, Right Worshipful Master of Lodge St David No. 36 and Councillor Ron Cairns of the City of Edinburgh Council. Lodge St David paid for the restoration of the painting. City of Edinburgh Collections, HH1638/1953.

By permission of the City of Edinburgh Council Museums Department.

First published in 2014 by Lomax Press, 13 Park Place, Stirling, Stirlingshire, FK7 9JR
Enquiries to info@lomaxpress.co.uk

For Peter

Contents

	Acknowledgements	8
	Preface	9
Chapter 1	Family Background	13
Chapter 2	Boyhood in the Pentland Hills	23
Chapter 3	Travels to London, Glasgow and the Continent	35
Chapter 4	Becoming Established in Edinburgh	47
Chapter 5	The Scott Monument	61
Chapter 6	Final Years in Edinburgh	77
Chapter 7	George Meikle Kemp's Legacy	95
Chapter 8	Afterword: Who was George Meikle Kemp?	109
Appendix:	Sources of Material Relating to George Meikle Kemp	113
	Bibliography	117
	Picture Credits	121
	Index	123

Acknowledgments

I am grateful to the staff of the following institutions: the Mitchell Library in Glasgow, Edinburgh Central Library, the Grand Lodge of Scotland, Archive Services of the University of Glasgow, Archives and Special Collections of the University of Strathclyde, Ayrshire Archives, the National Galleries of Scotland, the National Library of Scotland and the National Archives of Scotland.

A number of individuals very kindly responded to requests for specific information or advice, including the late John McKean, Deborah Mays, Joe Rock, Sara Stevenson, Brian Lambie, Anne Cameron, Scott Robertson, David Patterson, David Kiltie and Rich Pettit. I am grateful to Paul McAuley for showing me the work of the Edinburgh Museum Collections Centre, to John Cheeseman for transcription of original text, and to Marie Gibb for genealogical expertise.

I would like to thank several people whose especial input I very much appreciate. Denise Brace made me aware of, and facilitated access to, the Kemp archive at the Writers' Museum, Edinburgh, and was unstinting in her time. Mark and Liz Leese, and Willis Pickard very kindly read drafts, as did Robin Houston who, as well as providing information from his archives, offered invaluable advice and encouragement throughout this project. Any errors are of course entirely my own.

I am grateful to Forbes Gibb of Lomax Press, Michiel van der Lugt of Omnis Partners and Becky Green for their expertise in designing and producing the book.

Finally I would like to thank my dear husband Peter Main, who has supported me (in the midst of his own biographical work on the Scottish writer Ruthven Todd) with almost unfailing patience and good humour.

Preface

Saturday, 15 August 1840, was declared a public holiday in Edinburgh. Vast crowds thronged into the city. Civic dignitaries (including the splendidly named Kintyre Pursuivant and Marchmont Herald), 2,000 Freemasons and 3,000 ladies and gentlemen attended, along with a myriad of ordinary residents of Edinburgh. Visitors arrived from all over Scotland, military bands entertained the assembled crowds and troops were on hand to keep order. The better off had purchased tickets for specially constructed wooden galleries set up in Princes Street Gardens; those less fortunate could be seen hanging out of balconies and even crowded onto the tops of buildings. The occasion for these unprecedented celebrations was the laying of the foundation stone of a massive building project, the construction of a monument to the great Scottish literary genius of the Romantic era, Sir Walter Scott. The day was considered so important that a time capsule – a very early example of its type – was deposited underneath the monument. *The Scotsman* noted that 'something unusual' was in the air.

It was a chance for the upper echelons of society to see and be seen, for civic and military groups to make their mark, and for tradesmen and workers to enjoy a day out. The mood of the crowd was described by Hugh Miller, the innovative self-taught geologist and essayist. In his role as editor of the Free Church newspaper *The Witness* he captured

> *...the laugh, half in ridicule, half in good nature, with which the crowd greeted every very gaudily dressed member, richer in symbol and obsolete finery than his neighbour.*

Miller suggested that the crowds were not unduly deferential to the more pompous celebrants and were intent on enjoying themselves, and it seems that there was something for everyone on this day, from aristocrat to humble workman. Central to the event was of course the late Sir Walter Scott – but another key figure was the architect of the monument, George Meikle Kemp, a shepherd's son who, until a few years previously, had been unknown to the public. He had caught the imagination of the people of Edinburgh by winning the competition to design the monument – which he had entered under a pseudonym – and was becoming a well-known character in the city.

Today the Victorian Gothic profile of the Scott Monument, towering 200 feet (61 metres) over Princes Street, is known all over the world and is one of the most frequently reproduced images of Edinburgh. Such was the celebrity of the monument, from the time of its construction 170 years ago onwards, that some feared that it might even eclipse the reputation of its memorialised subject. Indeed, George Meikle Kemp became a celebrity himself: after his death memorials to him began to appear in places with which he had been associated, he was used as a case study in *Self Help* (the 19th century book by Samuel Smiles which advocated hard work and personal responsibility) and a club, meeting even today in the premises of the Scotch Malt Whisky Society, was named after him. A biography of him in the late 19th century by his nephew Thomas Bonnar presented some key facts about his life but at the same time created a kind of myth – that of the genius of lowly birth who triumphs against all odds. As is often the case with such myths, many wanted to claim an association with him, however remote: his name began to be associated with artworks and buildings, and family relationships were asserted, not always accurately.

My own interest in George Meikle Kemp was prompted by a family connection (my great-great-grandmother was his sister Violet and a piece of his furniture had pride of place in our home). I wondered what he was like as a person, and I was intrigued by rumours about the circumstances of his death. But initially my main thought was to try to locate examples of his architecture other than the Scott Monument. Surely an architect with an entry in the *Dictionary of National Biography* would have a corpus of work to view? And why was he known as a 'watercolourist? Where were his paintings? As it has turned out, I have been surprised at how little is left to represent his architectural output, apart from the monument: world-class in its impact but seemingly a one-off. His artistic works, fine though they are, are not large in number and are mainly pen-and-ink drawings, not watercolours. However, while his professional output was smaller than I expected, his life turned out to be fascinating, demonstrating a huge level of self-belief and drive, combined with a very unusual personality. He was marked by social disabilities, perhaps engendered by his humble background and exacerbated by a strange, almost autistic, personality. Despite his problems, he gained what the distinguished architectural historian Howard Colvin has described as a 'knowledge of Gothic architecture unrivalled in Scotland' and he came to inspire love and respect from those who knew him. This book is an account of his life.

Chapter 1
Family Background

George Meikle Kemp was born to a shepherding family in the south of Scotland on 25 May 1795. Figure 1 shows the places along the Pentland Hills where he lived during his childhood. He was the second son of James Kemp and Jean Mowbray who had married in 1790. His older brother Thomas had been born in 1792. Thomas and George had four younger sisters: Janet, Jane (or Jean), Isobel (or Isabella) and finally Violet, born in 1805, later Mrs Aitchison of Kilmory, Lochgilphead. It was she who provided the memories of George's childhood that his nephew Thomas Bonnar later drew on for his biography published in 1892. Some of her descendants also recorded memories about George, which they heard directly from her.

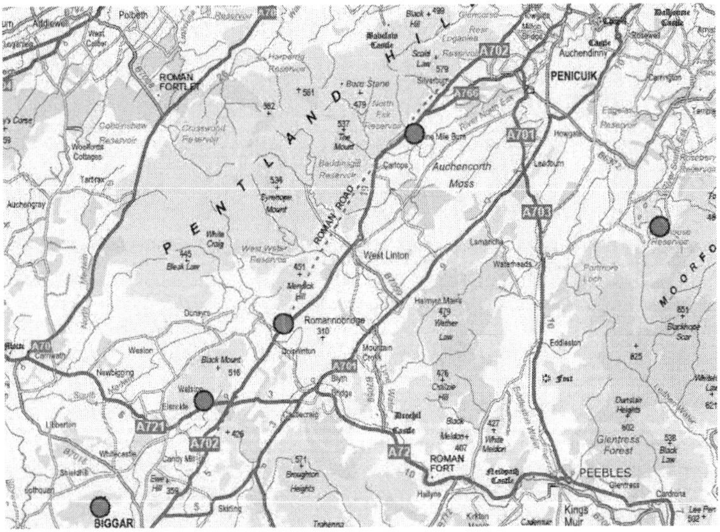

1 Map showing George Meikle Kemp's origins in the south of Scotland (approximate positions). Carnwath, Walston and Libberton, origins of his ancestors, are in the south west corner. Hillriggs, his birthplace, is just north of Biggar. His childhood homes followed the line of the Pentland Hills, where his father James was a shepherd, the final being Moorfoot at Gladhouse Loch, on the edge of the Moorfoot Hills.

George's father James is often said to have been born in 1767[1] but Robin Houston, a descendant of James, has provided strong evidence that he was actually born in 1754 to John Kemp and Janet (Pender), as recorded in the Old Parochial Registers of Biggar. This ancestry has been passed down, according to archives of the Houston family, to Jane Margaret Aitchison who died in 1956; she had this information from her aunt Isobel, John's granddaughter. John and Janet married in 1750 in Libberton in Lanarkshire, where John is described as being 'of Libberton' when he married, and his bride Janet as daughter of a 'portioner' – the owner of a small piece of land divided between heritors. The witnesses to the wedding were tenant farmers; Janet may thus have been slightly above the lowest level of society, but John had no occupation or status against his name in the banns and it is therefore likely that he was a labourer of some sort. Certainly there is no evidence that he was a 'well-to-do tenant farmer' as described by Bonnar, although he may have improved his position over time, particularly if he benefited in some way from his wife's family. We can at least be sure that the family into which James was born was not wealthy.

Pinpointing the birthplace of George's father James has been difficult. One of his daughters said in a letter to D.W. Kemp (an antiquarian interested in the Kemps but not directly related to George) that she always associated him with the village of Temple, Midlothian, and he is buried at Channelkirk, Oxton, not far away in the Borders. Temple has been the home of Kemps for many generations but notwithstanding this possible connection to the east, the origin was more likely to be near Biggar in Lanarkshire, where George was almost certainly born and where there were several Kemp families. The records of the Associate Congregation of Biggar between 1767 and 1798 include several Kemps: a Violet and a Jean of Whinbush, and two called James, from Whitecastle and Walston respectively. The Whitecastle James may have been George's father, and Violet and Jean may have been James' sisters, George's aunts.

1 See www.kempfamilyhistory.com for example.

Given James' background, Bonnar's claim that one George's paternal uncles was a lawyer who became a respected member of Dingwall society is a mystery. There certainly was an Alexander Kemp, Writer to the Signet (a private society of Scottish solicitors), who meets this description, but the records show no hint of any relationship between him and James. Among D.W. Kemp's archival material are tracings of signatures of brothers Donald and Hugh Kemp from 1750, Alexander Kemp from 1762, and finally James Kemp, shepherd at Moorfoot and Kemp's father, from 1820. It seems that D.W. Kemp believed that the first three Kemps, who were from Dingwall, and James were related. The north-east of Scotland had been home of a branch of Kemps since the 16th century, and perhaps he was trying to establish some kind of link (where none exists) with the southern Kemps. Another of James' brothers was said by Bonnar to be a doctor who had studied at Glasgow University. There is, however, no such person in the matriculation lists of the period, and there are only two matriculated Kemps (William and James, sons of the horticulturalist Andrew Kemp of Kirkurd). Again they seem not to have any connection with James' family. Doctors did not have to be qualified or registered until the mid-19th century so it is not surprising that we have no official records of a medical uncle, but one would have expected some other evidence, such as family recollections of such a person.

Bonnar's biography hints that George's father James was simply too lazy to avail himself of educational opportunities, such as the supposed uncles had received. On the other hand, one of James' granddaughters (Violet's daughter) said that he had been pressed into military service and was too old to learn a craft at discharge. We shall probably never know exactly why he became a shepherd but probably it was simply the only option given his background. Despite his poverty, he clearly provided for his family and ensured that they were educated. We might imagine that he was a genial man, from his appearance in Figure 2. Assuming that this portrait was made from life after George had married (and had to some extent made his name) James would have been aged around about 80 when he was painted. Although he indicates his humble shepherding background through his shepherd's maud in Borders tartan, his clothing is relatively formal; he had probably benefited by that time from his sons' success (and indeed Thomas was paying for James' keep towards the end of the latter's life.)

2 *James Kemp* (by William Bonnar). James was George Meikle Kemp's father. He is wearing the 'maud' or plaid in the so-called 'Borders' tartan, a simple check design that was a trademark of his occupation as a Borders shepherd. The artist was Kemp's brother-in-law and an early member of the Royal Scottish Academy.

George's mother Jean was born in 1764 and was buried in the parish of Walston. Her maiden name was Mowbray (a name with variants, e.g. Moubrey, Mubrie and Mulberry). Frederick Hitchin-Kemp, the early 20th century Kemp family historian, described George's mother as 'gifted and accomplished'. Although this statement was made without any particular justification, it is likely that she was jointly responsible with James for the foundation of George's education at home until he went to school aged six. Jean's father Thomas (born about 1740 in Carnwath) married Isobel Braidwood (born 1734 in Libberton) in 1760 in Walston. She may have had middle class connections: her sister Margaret Boag (née Braidwood) has been cited by family historians as first cousin-once-removed of Thomas Braidwood, the Covington-born pioneer of deaf education. This connection is backed up by a Mowbray descendant in a letter of 1910 to Gilbert Rae (an antiquarian of Penicuik who took an interest in George's life) and accords with Bonnar's claim of a relationship. The Braidwood family was notable in a number of fields. As well as their involvement with deaf education, Braidwoods were instrumental in setting up the modern fire service (in both the UK and the USA).

George's birthplace has been a matter of debate. No births to a James Kemp are recorded for 1795 in the pre-1855 parish registers. Ten years later James did baptise his daughter Violet in Penicuik, but registration was not a legal requirement in Scotland until 1855. Births outside the established Church of Scotland would not appear in official records, and James and Jean were members of the Associate Congregation in Biggar, a Presbyterian Church which had seceded from the Church of Scotland. An early biography of George (*Chambers's Edinburgh Journal*, 21 April 1838), based on Kemp's own words, states that he was 'reared' in Newhall but it did not state that he was born there.

Bonnar claimed that the birthplace was Moorfoot, a now deserted village near Gladhouse Loch (currently a reservoir and source of Edinburgh's water). However, in May - June 1910 there was a flurry of interest in the birthplace generated by a letter in *The Scotsman*, which cited a previous claim that Hillrigs (now Hillriggs), just outside Biggar (grid reference NT 029 393) was the birthplace. Against this, the Rev. J.C. Carrick, minister of Newbattle, presented the testimony of an old shepherd, a Mr Alves, who claimed to know that Moorfoot was the birthplace and that this had been confirmed by two emigrant farmer brothers from New Zealand whose father had stated the same thing. This was all part of a campaign to persuade public opinion that a monument to Robert Burns at the other end of Princes Street would be a fitting companion to that of Walter Scott, and to suggest that Lord Rosebery (who owned the estate on which Moorfoot lay) might foot the bill.

However, the claim that Moorfoot was George's birthplace was disputed further. D.W. Kemp's archive contains a letter dated 1920 from Thomas Bonnar, son of the biographer, saying that he was in fact not sure about the Moorfoot birthplace. Gilbert Rae referred, in letters to D.W. Kemp, to George's birthplace at 'a clump of trees beyond which the sun goes down' which could be seen from the tower of the old Secession Church of Biggar. This description would fit with the view in an early 20th century postcard of Kemp's birthplace held by the National Archives of Scotland. Rae also stated that he had heard from a Mowbray descendant whose grandmother had been present at the birth in Hillriggs. His birthplace is now accepted to be Hillriggs, largely based on evidence gathered by Brian Lambie and Robin Houston. It was at nearby Biggar that George's anniversary was celebrated in 1995, and there is now a memorial plaque overlooking Burn Braes Park, Biggar, set up by the Biggar Museum Trust. The modern farmhouse at Hillriggs is shown in Figure 3.

3 The view from the modern farm at Hillriggs (now called Hillridge), looking towards Biggar. Previously thought to be at Moorfoot, the place of George Meikle Kemp's birth on 25 May 1795 is now accepted as being Hillriggs, probably at a steading just behind the farm on the hillside. The National Archives of Scotland holds a postcard, probably from the early 20th century, showing a clump of trees, its only remaining trace by then.

Where did George's middle name 'Meikle' come from? Gilbert Rae thought that it was a tribute to Dr James Meikle of Carnwath, minister and army surgeon. He was locally celebrated and was famously broad-minded about others' faiths, even his wife's Antiburgher faith. The Burgher and Antiburgher churches were the products of the many and complicated splits from the Church of Scotland; both were Presbyterian, but had different views of the roles of Church and State. The Kemp family belonged to the 'Burgher' variety. Meikle was a man of high regard in the area and it is possible that he acted as elder for Hillriggs as well as Carnwath. The Kemps were religiously committed; according to Bonnar, they initially conceived the idea that George should train for the ministry, so the theory that Dr Meikle was the source of the name is at least plausible, particularly if he had acted as their medical adviser as well.

There is, however, evidence that Meikle was a family name, and official records confirm family connections. Agnes Tait, a great-great-granddaughter of James Kemp, said that her grandmother's brother was called David Meikle Johnston, and his mother said she had named him Meikle after an uncle of hers – the husband of her father's sister Jean. There was a marriage (in 1789) between Jean Kemp and George Muckle (as it was spelled), tanner and gluemaker, in Glasgow. Furthermore, a letter from Agnes Tait to D.W. Kemp states that a son of her uncle by marriage, Mr Meikle, married a Miss Steel; the marriage is probably that between Elizabeth Steel and David Meikle, skinner, recorded in 1834. This David Meikle may be the glue manufacturer of Spoutmouth and Little Dovehill, Glasgow who is recorded in *The Post-Office Glasgow Annual Directory* for 1843-44.

The Jean Kemp who may have been George's aunt is recorded in the Biggar church records in the early 80s, but not thereafter, and it is plausible that she moved to Glasgow for employment, and similarly George Meikle may well have come to work in the Tanwork Company in the Gallowgate. The Tanwork Company was one of the most successful businesses in Glasgow at the end of the 18th century and would have attracted many of the economic migrants at this time of Glasgow's first population explosion. Figure 4 shows Spoutmouth, off the Gallowgate, as it was in the early 19th century. Intriguingly there is a shop front in this image with 'Steel' above it, the name of the wife of George's putative cousin. It is possible that that George stayed in his youth with his Glaswegian family when he came to live in Glasgow (possibly studying at Anderson's Institution or at Robert Scott's Architectural Academy, both of which were close by).

4 Engraving of medieval buildings, now demolished, on the north side of Gallowgate, near Spoutmouth (Glasgow). Kemp's uncle by marriage, George Meikle, a glue manufacturer, lived here. George Meikle Kemp may have stayed with his Glaswegian family when he came to study, perhaps at Anderson's Institution or at Robert Scott's Architectural Academy, both a short distance from Spoutmouth.

Chapter 2
Boyhood in the Pentland Hills

George's father James Kemp was a cottar, that is, a peasant who lived in a cottage on another's land in return for work (perhaps in a building such as that shown in Figure 5). His living arrangements would have been to some extent at the mercy of his tenant farmer employer and he would often have been forced to move in order to find employment. This is the probable reason for the move of the family around the day of George's birth, which was near the Whitsunday Term day, a traditional time for re-employment. Indeed, Bonnar's story goes that James and his family had to move on the very day of his birth because his existing employer wished to re-open ancient lead mines in the area. Whether or not this story is true we shall probably never know (Bonnar sets this story in Moorfoot, rather than Hillriggs which was probably in fact his birthplace). However, cottars were regularly dispossessed so his family may well have had to move for some reason of this kind.

Old Farmhouse, Moorfoot.

5 *Old Farmhouse at Moorfoot* (by James Heron). One of several line drawings in Thomas Bonnar's biography of George Meikle Kemp. The village, on the edge of Gladhouse Loch, is now abandoned. This would have been typical of Kemp's childhood homes. He wrote a touching elegy from here in 1820, on seeing his father at his mother's grave.

It seems that a few days' grace was allowed and the family moved just after the birth. One of the Mowbray relatives gave a detailed account of the subsequent movements of the family during George's boyhood – starting at Newlanddale near Elsrickle, then in 1802 to Alleryburn at Mendick Foot near West Linton, in 1805 to Habbie's Howe on the Newhall estate near Carlops, and thence to Moorfoot when George was 12. These places all lie along the valley to the south of the Pentland Hills, as shown in Figure 1 (on page 14).The insecurity of life for a tenant farmer's employee comes across from David Kerr Cameron's description of their life in his book about farmtouns (collections of farm buildings) in the north-east of Scotland, *The Ballad and the Plough*:

> *The cottar folk of the farmtouns travelled light. Each year, usually at the Whitsunday Term but sometimes the Martinmas Term one as well, they threw their pitifully-few possessions into a farm cart and took the road to a new toun, like pilgrims to a promised land. Few in fact travelled hopefully for the years had taught them better, but in time the May 'flitting' became an addiction, a rootless custom of a rootless society.*

It may be that a Borders shepherd had a slightly higher social status and income than the cottars described by Cameron, because of the economic importance of sheep in southern Scotland. West Linton (where James Kemp eventually settled) was the focal point for sheep trading to the Highlands: it even had a new breed of black-faced sheep, the Linton, named after it. Nevertheless, it is clear that the Kemp family was on the move, albeit within a relatively small area, and their lifestyle must have been somewhat impoverished. Indeed, according to Gilbert Rae, the Kemps had applied for parish relief from Walston Parish, and there is a parish record referring to such payments to a Kemp family. George was certainly born in relatively straitened circumstances, and later in life was to describe the family's forced move with some bitterness, remembering his mother weeping on saying goodbye to her cherished cottage garden with its medicinal herbs. On a positive note, he would have had the psychological challenge of adapting himself to several new environments. In the first ten years of his life he lived in four homes and attended three schools: this would have undoubtedly contributed to the remarkable resilience and independence of mind that would emerge later in his life.

George also benefited from a basic but sound Scottish education. Scotland's educational provision at that time was relatively widespread, and may be said to have underpinned the Scottish Enlightenment and the industrial revolution in Scotland. By the end of the 18th century, most parishes would have had a school, and according to William Hunter in his local history of 1827, *Biggar and the House of Fleming*:

> *It is a rare thing for a child of any of the settled inhabitants to grow up without receiving, at least, the rudiments of education. From time to time, Biggar schools have sent forth not a few pupils, who have, in after years, become clergy men, surgeons, lawyers, authors, editors, etc.*

The New Statistical Account for Scotland (referring to Lanarkshire in 1828) mentions a parochial school at Walston, and one at nearby Elsrickle on the site of the Antiburgher Church (which had disbanded by that time). These schools were supported partly by fees and partly by the heads of families, and the curriculum included reading, writing, arithmetic, geography and algebra, with a few learning Latin. Local people raised funds for a library in the area by subscription in 1828. Although this evidence refers to some 15 or 20 years after George's childhood, it nevertheless attests to the commitment to education and self-improvement of the people of this area.

In the latter part of his school career, George had conventional teachers. In West Linton he studied under John Mossman, father of the sculptor William Mossman and grandfather of John Mossman, also a renowned sculptor and founder of the Glasgow School of Art, and he attended Penicuik School while living in Moorfoot. Before this he was taught, along with his cousin John Aitken, at the elementary school in Walston by a local eccentric, Adam Thomson. According to William Hunter, Thomson had spent some time as an amateur sleuth avenging the death of his father, who had been murdered by gypsies. By mixing with low-life all over Scotland and England he was able to call the perpetrators to book, and as they were being hanged in the Grassmarket, Edinburgh, Thomson mounted the gallows himself to offer up a prayer. He was well known in the Biggar area and regarded as a figure of fun. He caused local amusement through his self-description as rector of the 'Academy of Walston' and in his rather poor Latin (translating 'Blacklaw, near Newbigging', by *Nigram Legem, prope Novam Edificationem*, for example).

Violet, George's youngest sister (shown later in life as Mrs Aitchison in Figure 6) provided testimony in Bonnar's biography on other aspects of George's early years. She described an idealised portrait of a bucolic life in which he would roam the hillsides while helping his father and a neighbouring farmer in Ninemileburn with shepherding. He had a pet dog, its somewhat unimaginative name of Dog indicating no disrespect to the animal kingdom, as Violet explained. Far from it: George was supposedly of the opinion that even the smallest of animals deserved consideration. However, his true interests were technical and intellectual. While herding, he would neglect 'his fleecy charges', as Bonnar puts it, in favour of the more interesting occupation of damming local burns to construct waterworks – the favourite activity of many a young boy and one which seems to have rather irritated his parents.

6 Violet Aitchison, née Kemp, photographed in Belfast in 1869. Violet was George Meikle Kemp's youngest sister. She provided interesting reminiscences of her brother, after moving to Argyll where she was an estate factor's wife. She lived in Northern Ireland for a time, and numbers Dame Elizabeth Blackadder among her many descendants.

The image Violet paints of her family's home life at that time is similar to that described in Robert Burns' poem *The Cotter's Saturday Night*, as depicted in Figure 7. The poem, with its depiction of a poor but spiritually rich family life, has come to symbolise Scottish rural life, and indeed pious family life everywhere. Allowing for the Victorian tendency to sentimentalise (and the fact that Violet was 10 years younger than her brother and may have had rose-tinted and inevitably rather fragmentary memories of that time), it gives a nice image of the young George in the warm and supportive environment of the poem. Certainly Violet did not mention their early privations, as George did in his later writings.

7 *The Cotters Saturday Night* (etching, stipple and engraving, after John Masey Wright). This is one of many representations of Burns' poem, which depicts a financially poor but spiritually rich family life. This is the image George Meikle Kemp's sister Violet presented of the Kemp family in her reminiscences of their early life.

In 1806, when he was ten years old, George visited Rosslyn Chapel and Roslin Castle, while on an errand for Mr Brown of the Newhall Estate. The chapel, which was built in 1446 for the foundation of an uncompleted collegiate church, was renowned then and now, especially following the 2006 film, *The Da Vinci Code*. Annie Wilson, the landlady of the Roslin Inn, was a self-appointed guide who had a reputation, reported in *The Gentleman's Magazine*, September 1817, for her witch-like appearance and for the stories with which she regaled visitors (many of whom were celebrated personalities, including Dr Samuel Johnson, Sir Walter Scott and William Wordsworth). One of these, The Apprentice Pillar story, concerns an apprentice who completes a complex design while his master travels to Rome to see the original, only to be murdered by the master on his return. This story, which appears in many guises over Europe as a warning to apprentices to know their place, would surely have made a deep impression on the young George, as would the staggeringly intricate carving in the chapel. Figure 8 shows an example of carving from the Eastern Aisle. It is intriguing

8 *Rosslyn Chapel* (etching after R. W. Billings). George Meikle Kemp first visited Rosslyn as a boy, when he would have heard the 'Apprentice Pillar' story about the apprentice murdered by a master jealous of his talents. He revisited the chapel as an adult, and both he and his son Thomas were involved in discussions on its restoration.

that George was to visit Europe to observe ancient architectural designs, which he later adapted to his own style, ultimately confounding his 'masters' – the architectural establishment of Edinburgh.

George's parents recognised that they had a son with talents which deserved development through further training and which might have been lost had he followed his father's footsteps as a shepherd or, for that matter, become a minister as they had hoped. According to Violet, his father said: 'We will have to make some other thing than a shepherd of George – the sheep or cows seem to be the least of his care'. Accordingly, after he left school aged 14, they enrolled him, in 1809, in an apprenticeship in joinery with Andrew Noble, master-wright and carpenter, at Moy Hall, Redscarhead (near Eddleston, a few miles north of Peebles). A memorial to George is situated there, commissioned by Peebles Burgh Council and designed by the architect James Grieve in 1932 on the one hundredth anniversary of the death of Sir Walter Scott (Figure 9).

9 Memorial to George Meikle Kemp at Noble's house and joinery at Redscarhead, Peebles. The joiners' grindstone is in front of the memorial. The apprentices lived and studied together in the 'Men's Room'. Kemp studied there as an apprentice during the week, and would walk home to his family at weekends, the start of his lifelong habit of walking everywhere.

George stayed with Noble until June 1813 and learnt the usual skills of joinery, including technical drawing, as well as mastering various mechanical skills while repairing farm machinery as part of his duties.

This latter activity was to equip him with skills of value to him in his first job as a millwright. He would walk the twelve miles home from his place of work on Saturday nights. This became a life-long habit: in later life he was to walk enormous distances in search of work or to study medieval buildings. Some aspects of his slightly eccentric personality come through from reminiscences of those who knew him at that time. At the Scott Centenary Celebration at Coldstream (*Berwickshire News*, 22 August 1871), Noble's son James was to recall his friend Geordie (George) asking him to come up with a plan to persuade a rather slothful and grubby colleague, Jamie Bell, to mend his ways. George presented the unfortunate Jamie with a drawing of a skull and cross-bones accompanied by an 'epitaph' which he had composed:

Here lies James Bell: a man of dubious worth;
Ere death from sloth his loathful carcase hurried,
His soul and body lived above the earth
While both of them were deep beneath it buried.

This was a bit rich coming from George, who was himself famously against any idea of 'putting on an appearance'. When he left Noble's workshop for his first job, James' sister tried to tidy him up, brushing his shoes only to have George dip them in water to remove the lustre, presumably because it would have made him look too smart.

In this period of his life he and his colleagues would have been exposed to practical geometry of the type shown in Figure 10, from a standard book, *The Carpenter's New Guide*, first published in 1792. Its author, Peter Nicholson, was a local boy from a remarkably similar background to George's, who invented draughtsman's instruments such as the centrolinear (used for perspective drawing) and wrote on architectural and mathematical topics. His publications show the level of mathematical sophistication demanded of architects and joiners of the time, occupations which required many skills in common. At Noble's workshop these skills were honed through practical work, and by private study in what was known as the 'Men's Room', where the apprentices lived and spent their leisure hours together.

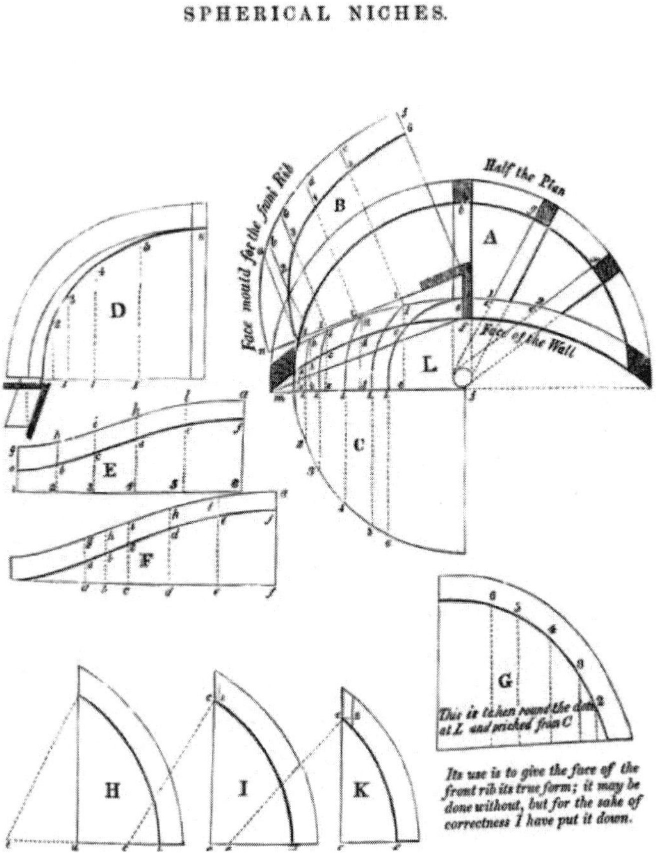

10 *Spherical Niches*, Plate XXXIII, from Peter Nicholson's *The Carpenter's New Guide*. This book, originally published in 1792, was a widely-used resource for joiners and architects, and covers the complex technical drawing skills that were required for these professions.

George did not neglect other aspects of his educational development at this time, which seems to have been for the most part self-directed. He was in the habit of carving cups or quaichs from oak found in the local peat moss, carving being a skill which greatly aided his later career since it allowed him to make three-dimensional wooden models with ease.

This was a practice which was already beginning to die out in the 19th century, although it had ancient origins and is attested from the Italian Renaissance. George was to become well known for his facility in this method of illustrating his concepts. He also cultivated the humanities: his writings of later years include some poetry, perhaps not to our modern taste but including many literary references with which he must have at least started to become familiar at that age. He also played the violin in later life, and again one must assume that he taught himself as a youth at a time when he could hardly have afforded music lessons.

Before turning to George's working life, one might reflect on his background influences. The Scottish Lowlands in the 18th and 19th centuries provided a seedbed for enormous intellectual and artistic achievement. It was into this rich cultural environment that George was born. Stewart Lamont's book *When Scotland Ruled the World* lists the many famous Scots of achievement born in that era. Among them, to mention just two, are the writer and satirist Thomas Carlyle and the engineer Thomas Telford. Like Carlyle, George was from a humble family of the Presbyterian 'Burgher' faith, and like Telford he was a shepherd's son; other examples could be cited. What do these sons of Scotland have in common? One feature of their upbringing, as Lamont claims, was 'a good education system and a religious climate in which speculation and intellectual enquiry were admired and not stifled.' Although George Meikle Kemp is routinely described as the 'self-taught' son of a shepherd, he left home with the inheritance of a sound education, and personal characteristics of resilience, independence of mind and determination. These were to stand him in good stead in the next – perambulatory – stage in his life, which was to begin on his discharge from the apprenticeship in June 1813.

Chapter 3
Travels to London, Glasgow and the Continent

In 1813, aged 18, George set off with his tool bag on the 18-mile journey from Moorfoot to start his first job in a carpenter's workshop at Roxburgh House Court, Galashiels. The workshop is no longer there but a commemorative plaque can be seen in the court, erected by the Abbotsford Scott Fellowship in 1935. He travelled by foot, as was his custom. Near Elibank Tower in Selkirkshire a kindly gentleman offered him a lift in his carriage, a mode of transport which was no doubt a great luxury for George. He was too shy to converse with his companion whose distinguished identity he only discovered afterwards: Walter Scott, then the 'Shirra' or Sherriff of Selkirkshire. Figure 11 shows Scott around this time, with his dog Camp. This was the first of two close encounters that George had with Scott. The second occurred while he was sketching Melrose Abbey: Scott was approaching when his dog Maida distracted his attention at the last minute and drew him away so that, as with his earlier contact, George failed to engage with the future subject of his memorial.

11 *Walter Scott Esq.* (mezzotint print, after Henry Raeburn). Walter Scott (not yet Sir Walter) is depicted in 1810 around the time when he would have given George Meikle Kemp a lift in his carriage on the road at Elibank Tower in Selkirkshire. Kemp remembered the event in later life; at the time he was too shy to engage in conversation.

The job that George had secured in Galashiels was that of millwright, an occupation that was concerned with much more than mill machinery, although that was its origin. In the early 19th century the technology of milling was extended to other industrial activities which were gradually being mechanised, initially using components made of wood and later of iron. Millwrights, among others, were thus forerunners of today's mechanical engineers, and men (such as George) with their skills were in demand for fixing all kinds of machinery. The job meant travelling around, and this gave ample opportunity to study and sketch the ecclesiastical buildings of the area, including the Abbeys of Melrose, Dryburgh and Jedburgh. George's method, according to Bonnar, was to study the general form of a building, and to make some detailed sketches of particular mouldings or decorative features, such as gargoyles, that interested him, but not to make plan drawings or views: he was able to commit these, and how the detailed parts fitted together, to memory. Many of these sketches are kept in the Kemp archive at the Writers' Museum in Edinburgh and demonstrate his celebrated ability for close observation.

A building which George studied in great depth, and to which he was to return later in life, was Melrose Abbey (shown in Figure 12 on the next page). This building was to become the artistic inspiration for the Scott Monument. Unusually for a building of the medieval period there is an inscription, in the south transept of the Abbey, by one of the master stonemasons responsible for its rebuilding in the 15th century (usually a mason's mark is all that is known of these craftsmen). This Parisian mason, John Morvo (Jean Moreau or John Morrow), was probably the master stonemason of a number of Scottish ecclesiastical buildings (mentioned in the inscription), to which he brought innovative French features. George clearly identified himself with this style of architecture and eventually adopted 'John Morvo' as his pseudonym.

In 1815 George moved closer to Edinburgh to work as a joiner in John Cousin's builder's workshop in Leith. John Cousin was the father of David Cousin who became a well-known architect himself. David com peted with George in the Scott Monument competition and was to be come a great friend, teaching architecture to George's son Thomas.

12 Melrose Abbey, founded in 1136 by King David I and rebuilt in 1385. It was the subject of a drawing and suggested restoration by George Meikle Kemp. It was source of his pseudonym 'John Morvo' (who was the Abbey's French master mason) and it was the inspiration for his design for the Scott Monument.

From 1813 onwards, the New Town of Edinburgh was being extended by the addition of the so-called 'Third New Town'. The area around William Street in the West End and the village of Stockbridge were being developed, and this part of Edinburgh would have been very much a building site. While it is from a slightly later date, Alexander Nasmyth's painting (Figure 13), looking from the West End down Princes Street to the eventual site of the Scott Monument, gives some idea of what it may have looked like, with all the bustle of materials being delivered. Working on these building sites as a joiner for John Cousin would have given George many opportunities for understanding the practicalities of converting architecture into buildings, as a complement to the knowledge of design that he had gained from his sketching activities.

In 1817 George left home once again and went to Lancashire, working as a carpenter there for three years. According to his sister Violet it was Manchester where he temporarily settled, and it is likely that George was attracted to that city because of the availability of construction work in the mills and associated back-to-back housing schemes for the workers, as well as in the mill-owners' villas. In his spare time he studied the great ecclesiastical buildings of the area, sometimes walking long distances to visit them, well over 60 miles in the case of York Minster. His next port of call was Glasgow, like Manchester a rapidly expanding city with opportunities for building workers. Here he was again successful in obtaining employment and over the next four years he continued to work, and study in the evenings. As in his boyhood, he benefited from the relatively advanced educational provision in Scotland, probably including studies at Anderson's Institution.

13 *Princes Street with the Commencement of the Building of the Royal Institution* 1825 (oil on canvas by Alexander Nasmyth). The street is shown with building materials being delivered, and a site hut. George Meikle Kemp had opportunities to observe and participate in building work during this period in the development of Edinburgh.

Founded in 1796 from a bequest by John Anderson, the college was remarkable in pioneering working-class education. It was one of the first colleges to provide evening classes, and the first to teach women on equal terms with men. It is one of the academic ancestors of the University of Strathclyde, which keeps the archives of the curricula offered. These were particularly designed to appeal to working men such as George, as they included practical subjects such as draughtsmanship, geometry and basic science and, crucially for the working man, were available in the evenings.

Like so many of his compatriots, George felt the need to try his luck in London, and in 1824 aged 29 he set out for the metropolis, staying there for a period of 13 months. He probably appeared rather uncouth to Londoners. A review of Bonnar's biography in *The Athenaeum*, 24 December 1892, describes George's manner (as it appeared in the examples of correspondence which Bonnar quoted) as 'cantankerous'. Opinionated might be a fairer description. The review also describes him as a

> *...shrewd, industrious, pushing Scotchman such as by their success in life away from home have become typical in the eyes of other nations.*

There is some truth in this description (except his designation as shrewd, which he certainly was not: rather, his friends described his 'childlike simplicity'). The description may have been prompted in part by a feeling of irritation with the Scots who, then as now, may have seemed to be taking over the English capital. However, despite George's skills and undoubted industry, which he might have hoped would attract employment opportunities in the rapidly expanding metropolis, he failed to find permanent work there. Perhaps his cantankerousness was just too much for the suave southerners.

George's failure in finding employment meant that, although enjoying visits to St Paul's and Canterbury Cathedrals, he was discontented. In a letter to a friend he says that his 'blinks of happiness, like those of the sun in that city were few and far between'. He even described London as a 'putrid spreading stain deforming nature's face' in his poem 'London', reproduced by Bonnar. He regarded London as a sink of luxury, and the contrast between the depravity of the wealthy aristocrat and the simple lifestyle of the working man was to become a constant theme for George, stemming from memories of his family's early privations. He was heartily contemptuous of the Scottish nobility's excesses which he saw as vain attempts to impress the English. He was particularly scandalized by the dandies consorting with, as it seemed to him, semi-naked ladies glimpsed through the open windows at society balls (such as that depicted in Figure 14). Needless to say, when confronted by such sights, as a conscientious Presbyterian he made his excuses and left.

14 *The Cyprian's Ball, at the Argyle Rooms,* from *The English Spy* by Bernard Blackmantle, 1825. According to letters George Meikle Kemp sent home from London, the scantily-dressed women at such balls were a source of outrage to the somewhat straight-laced Kemp, as was the evident extravagance of the upper classes.

Having failed to find work in London, he decided to go to France and Belgium, primarily in order to study medieval architecture. When asked by a workmate in Leith, to which he had briefly returned, how he expected to get there, Bonnar has him replying:

> *I hae a croon, something else forbye – ye ken I can always take a turn of work on the road, and I hae nae fear but I will get on all right.*

This attitude indicates an underlying self confidence, especially in view of his failure to find employment in London and his inability to speak the language. He did attempt to learn some French and in exchange for these lessons introduced his French colleagues to Scots expressions such as 'hallanshaker' (tramp). He may have at times seemed to be a hallanshaker himself, since as an itinerant worker he had to live from hand-to-mouth and was prepared, even keen, to sleep rough. A glimpse of his life on the road was provided by an Italian artist, Felice Pitconie, whose remarks were recorded by a lady in Elgin who got into conversation with him while he was drawing the Cathedral. Describing him as 'that leetle man with short trousers', he recalled bumping into George in France, each giving the other a nasty surprise since both had been engaged in illicitly scrumping for apples.

George considered his time on the continent to be a success, more so than he had expected; this was possibly the result of his skills as a millwright which were much in demand in France at that time. He spent several months in Boulogne and visited the magnificent Gothic church of St Vulfran at Abbeville, the cathedrals of Beauvais and Amiens and the Church of St Geneviève in Paris. Visiting Belgium, he would have studied Antwerp Cathedral whose spire, shown in Figure 15, was later said by his detractors to have been the model for the Scott Monument, some even accusing him of direct plagiarism.

Letters back home to his brother and friends during these sojourns abroad describe his success or otherwise in finding work, and include comments on local architecture and somewhat rambling accounts of his attitude to life, along with greetings to friends (the latter often in Scots). One of these letters, an extract of which is shown in Figure 16 (see page 44), is interesting in revealing his state of mind. The passage shown there is preceded by an account of a night spent sleeping

15 *View of the Cathedral of Our Lady in Antwerp* (etching by J. Linnig, 1846). George Meikle Kemp visited Antwerp in Belgium when on his Continental tour, as well as Northern France and Paris. This building influenced his design for the Scott Monument (and some even accused him of plagiarising it).

in a cave during a storm, where he encounters a radiant form, who commands him to 'tell your fellows what you have seen and heard if they believe they will renew their energy and gain the hapy [sic] shore'. He then goes on to describe

> *...a great dome with a wide and shiny chamber appearing in the top and that opening filled with a horograph wheel containing three hundred and sixty five spokes on one side so broad as almost to exclude the light and gradually diminishing toward the other till they almost lost their shadow if this wheel were moved so slowly about as to make only once round in the course of a year the light and shadow of the spokes on a certain point on the pavement below would correspond exactly with day and night through the year but if it were to fly around with the fury of lightning the light and darkness would be so completely blended as to produce nearly a glimmering vapour...*

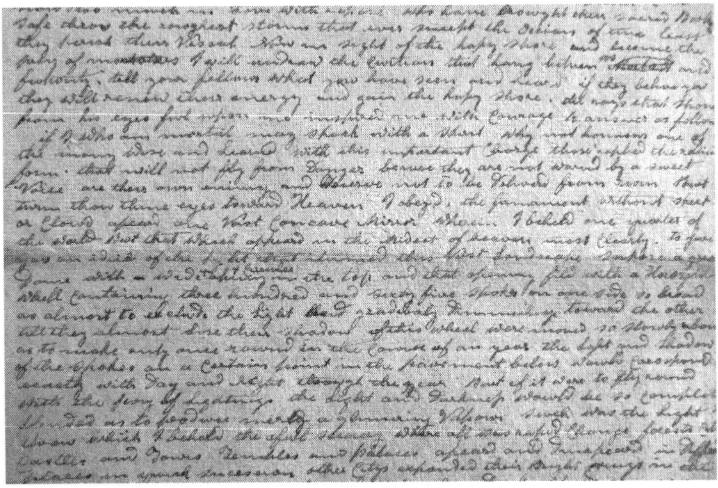

16 Extract from a letter by George Meikle Kemp. This was one of several letters and other texts, written to his friends and his brother when travelling to London and the Continent, which indicate Kemp's extraordinary imagination. Other writings include poems (some very lengthy), descriptions of local customs or the built environment, and reminiscences of the difficult circumstances of his youth.

The letter continues in an impenetrable style with accounts of apocalyptic visions such as

> *...constant roar of thunder filled the air volcanos burst from mountain tops every mountain pouring their melted bowels down their seething sides...*

The description of the enormous horological device suggests that even at that stage in his life he was, perhaps subconsciously, mulling over ideas of creating large-scale edifices.

Tellingly the passage is not quoted by Bonnar, unlike much of the material in his other letters: perhaps it seemed to Bonnar to be fuelled by opium or alcohol or, even more worryingly, by some kind of mental illness. External sources for George's strange landscape visions can be conceived. For example, they may have been manifestations of what the Scottish scientist John Playfair described in the *Transactions of the Geological Society* of 1811-12 as 'a species of mental derangement, in which the patient raved continually of comets, deluges, volcanoes and earthquakes' (the 'patient' here refers to the typical amateur student of geology). Another possibility is that it comes from biblical reading, with the wheel which features in the 'Inaugural Vision' of Ezekiel being transformed into the colossal clock. Finally, the idea of the heavens opening to reveal a vision may have been inspired by the *Storms* by James Hogg ('the Ettrick Shepherd'). This was a popular article in *Blackwood's Magazine* which was reprinted several times and which George would have had the opportunity to read. Whatever its origins, it seems that George had decided to resolve the vision into a more socially acceptable form through the medium of poetry. A rambling poem of 104 stanzas and at least 5,000 words, entitled 'The Dream' (which Bonnar does reproduce) reworks some of these images.

After visiting Belgium, George hurried back to Scotland. According to Bonnar, the return was prompted by the death of his mother but this seems unlikely. For one thing, family tradition (passed down from his sister Violet) would put his mother's death much earlier, around 1817, when Violet was still a child; this is confirmed by the existence of a poem written by George in Moorfoot, dated 1820, which refers to his mother's grave. Furthermore, a report much closer in time (and based on George's own words from *Chambers's Edinburgh Journal*, 21 April 1838, explains that his return was due to the 'commercial embarrassments of a near relative'. We do not know who this relative might have been but the word 'commercial' might suggest the involvement of his brother Thomas, rather than his father. There is a reference to Thomas from a few years later in a House of Commons Report of the Select Committee on Fictitious Votes in Scotland of 1837, where it was suggested that, among many others, he had participated in a vote-rigging scam on large Scottish estates whereby the number of eligible voters was increased through fake house purchase. It seems that Thomas had 'form' in engaging in dubious commercial activities.

George returned to Scotland for good; he had abandoned his idea of emigrating to Canada, as he had at one time intended (being an admirer of North America as remarks in his letters show). His next task was to make a living at the craft of joinery. His life had, so far, been a mixed success financially but since he could support himself and study ancient buildings he was content. He was well on his way to attaining 'a first-hand knowledge of Gothic architecture unrivalled in Scotland', as the architectural historian Howard Colvin has put it. However, his self-taught architectural knowledge could not provide him with sustenance. Since life as a journeyman was precarious he resolved to try to make a living as an independent businessman. He accordingly moved back to Edinburgh, to Roxburgh Close off the Royal Mile, describing himself there as a cabinet maker.

Chapter 4
Becoming Established in Edinburgh

Finally settled in Edinburgh, George renewed contact with his friends James Noble, David Cousin and others. A significant event for his social life was his initiation in 1827 into St Andrew's Masonic Lodge, No. 48, Edinburgh. Freemasonry started in Medieval Scotland as an organisation for stonemasons, whose knowledge of geometry gave them an exclusive status they wished to protect. The moneyed classes without any particular craft connection began to join the movement during the 18th century, and were especially welcome if they could contribute funds. Freemasons were socially powerful and almost always involved in the major public works of Edinburgh. Membership of a Lodge would thus have allowed access to a wide network of contacts, now that it was composed of all classes of Edinburgh society. George was a representative of the older type of craft member, and in place of the normal fees he constructed the Master's Chair, which was restored after it had become dilapidated by Thomas Bonnar; it still stands in the Lodge St Andrew. (George was also enrolled in the Lodge of Journey-Men Masons, No. 8, Edinburgh but this was much later, in 1843).

The possibility of an intriguing Masonic connection is contained in a frankly adulatory letter dated 1828, including an acrostic on the name George Kemp, which was left by an anonymous admirer and found in his papers after his death:

Genius, that attribute divine
Enjoyned with Sense, is truly thine
Oft, as thy works by man are seen,
Refulgent rays of Taste will then
Gain inroads on thy soul, and teach
Enticing lessons, but to reach
Keen as the mind may be, thy sphere
Even with thy aid, few could apply
May Heaven, from every storm
Preserve thee till thy dying hour.

The letter was addressed to George Kemp, cabinet maker, and at one point talks of the 'ten degrees of criticism' – does this reference to 'degrees' suggest a fellow Freemason as author? Or given George's predilection for composing poetry and his fertile imagination could we imagine him even writing it himself? The 'refulgent rays' and reference to a storm are reminiscent of the 'visions' passage described earlier. Perhaps both theories are far-fetched; but whoever the author is, the letter is rather mysterious.

George was clearly very talented in joinery, as shown by his furniture, several examples of which survive. An example of one of his more workmanlike pieces is shown in Figure 17a; other more delicate and intricate pieces, such as the example in Figure 17b, come onto the antiques market from time to time and can command a high price. A bookcase-bureau made by George is on display at the Writers' Museum.

17 (a) Chest of drawers made by George Meikle Kemp (b) bookcase attributed to Kemp. The first is a workmanlike piece which was kept in the family, with a plan drawer at the top and deep drawers; the second a more decorative object.

George was also employed at one stage (it is not clear when) to make miniature wooden models of military medical equipment, such as field ambulances, for the Professor of Military Surgery at Edinburgh University, Sir George Ballingall. These were listed in the catalogue of Ballingall's Museum of Military Surgery prepared in 1843-44 by students but sadly the display came to be dispersed in recent times. (The Anatomy Department at the Old Medical School of the University of Edinburgh held some of the exhibits until recently, but not these models). George was well known for his wood-turning skills and, as a fellow wright recounted, once took the opportunity to create a wooden hat for himself. When required to turn an oval, the remaining wood made the hat, which he then covered to form what was described as 'serviceable and becoming headgear'. Despite these skills, George failed to establish himself as an independent carpenter and joiner. Various events in his life, and comments by others, suggest that this was probably due to his character – he was not noted for his business acumen or ability to promote himself.

Draughtsmanship was in any case more to his taste than joinery and his reputation in this area was gradually increasing. He made a special journey to Melrose and drew three views of the Abbey which attracted much admiration and were exhibited in the Scottish Academy Exhibition of 1830, later being bought by the architect Thomas Hamilton. The fine quality of his draughtsmanship can be seen in Figure 18. His aim in this drawing was to suggest a restoration of the original building in the most authentic way he could, not to create something new – this was to come later. Interestingly, his explanation of his motivation for the Melrose drawing was given in Alexander Whitelaw's 1833 compendium *The Republic of Letters*:

> *In attempting a restored view of Melrose Abbey, my aim has been to adhere strictly to the original details...the west tower, slightly seen in the distance, and part of the spire, are the only parts for which I have not sufficient data.*

George's use of the word 'data', by which he meant the remains of the medieval building combined with the knowledge he had acquired of Gothic architecture generally, indicates that he was, in the early part of the 1830s, thinking of himself primarily as a kind of archaeologist or art historian.

18 *Melrose Abbey (Restored)* (by G. M. Kemp, engraved by James Johnstone). George Meikle Kemp's three drawings of Melrose made his name as an architectural artist and provided some money (they were bought by the architect Thomas Hamilton). A comment by Kemp on this drawing indicates that at that time his interests were primarily restorative and antiquarian rather than creative.

Although George was reported to have been well paid for the Melrose drawings he needed a steady source of income, not just one-off payments. Fortunately his brother Thomas, who was clerk of works for the Duke of Buccleuch, was able to assist his career by securing a job for him with the architect William Burn on the Duke's estate at Bowhill, Selkirk, preparing drawings for the new house to be built there. In 1831 he was commissioned to make a model in wood of Burn's design for a new palace on the Dalkeith estate, which was also owned by the Duke of Buccleuch. This work occupied George and an assistant for two years, but despite the massive effort that this involved, like so many of George's projects the model had no ultimate purpose other than as a greatly-admired decorative object. In this case it was because, through none of his fault, the building itself never materialised and was eventually built to a different design. The magnificent model has been withdrawn from public display at Bowhill due to changes there but it is anticipated that in the long term it will again be on display, at Dalkeith Estate.

George's brother Thomas is a rather shadowy figure: there are no reminiscences about his childhood from Violet as there are for George. In 1825 he was described as a joiner but later became a clerk of works. The few pieces of evidence about him include the Parliamentary Committee report mentioned earlier, and *The Journal of Building Work at Dalkeith and Caroline Park from 1829-1831* (part of the Duke of Buccleuch's archive). Although unsigned, it is catalogued by the National Archives of Scotland as possibly by Thomas. There are also references to him in the diaries of John Smith of Darnick, also in the Archives. Smith, a prolific builder and architect who worked, among other projects, on Sir Walter Scott's home Abbotsford House, describes him as arriving from Edinburgh in September of 1831 as 'Burn's man' to work for the Duke of Buccleuch. Having later worked in Knowsley, Lancashire, for a short time (again for Burn) Thomas returned to Edinburgh. He was in bad health and was to die in Dalkeith on 24 May 1841. He remained close to George, as their correspondence shows.

Around this time George made the acquaintance in Edinburgh, through his employer John Cousin, of William Bonnar, decorator and heraldic painter and latterly portrait painter, of West Port (later of London Street). In addition to a daughter Elizabeth, whom George was to marry, Bonnar had three sons, William, Thomas and Dundas; William junior was a successful painter, specialising initially in rural scenes and children and later in portraits, and was one of the founder members of the Royal Scottish Academy. Figure 19 is a print based on one of his paintings showing the Duchess of Buccleuch, in the role of a gracious lady visiting a humble family, probably in similar circumstances to those of George's own parents. It was William's son Thomas who wrote his uncle George's biography.

George's friendship with Bonnar paid social dividends, not only in the form of a future wife but also introductions to a number of luminaries of the Edinburgh artistic scene, including James Drummond, the historical painter and antiquarian, and George Harvey who was to become President of the Royal Scottish Academy.

19 *The Benefactresses Elizabeth Duchess of Buccleuch & Harriet Countess of Dalkeith Visiting a Widow's Cottage* (print by Thomas Dick, after William Bonnar, 1839). The interior gives an indication of what George Meikle Kemp's own background might have been like. The Duke of Buccleuch had been Kemp's employer for a time, when he assisted William Burn at Bowhill House, Selkirk.

George was by all accounts a very shy and somewhat strange young man. His work-mates had noticed a tendency for him to work in complete silence for days at a time and to make sudden unannounced sketching trips. He certainly must have cut an odd figure at times, as one of Bonnar's anecdotes illustrates. In preparing for a Committee (for the restoration of Glasgow Cathedral) he was aware that he was somewhat travel-stained, having walked from Edinburgh to Glasgow. He ended up putting on a clean shirt front but forgetting to remove the old one. Another tale was told by a friend who, while chatting to him in the street, noticed that George's arm started to move apparently under its own steam. His arm was making jerking movements as if to practise the act of shaking hands; seemingly he had spotted an acquaintance in the distance. Eventually George was able to complete the handshake with obvious mental relief. His friend also noted that his shyness was combined with a tendency to 'go on a bit' once started on a topic close to his heart and this is very evident from his letters to friends from abroad. As George put it himself in one of these letters, his mind was 'like a thick fiddle, it requires hard playing upon before the music flows freely'.

Clearly he got over his famous diffidence sufficiently to propose marriage to Elizabeth Bonnar. However, according to Bonnar, George blotted his copybook several times while they were engaged. On one occasion he took her on a trip to his previous home at Newhall. He managed to miss the coach back to Edinburgh, probably (according to Bonnar) while waxing lyrical on the subject of his old home and plans to build a house for the two of them. Elizabeth was understandably not happy about the prospect of walking the 13 miles back home. Bonnar further relates the story of a volume of the New Testament which George had presented to Elizabeth, with his own design on the front and a rather touching verse dedicated to her. This verse was cut out after a quarrel, but restored later, and they married on 11 September 1832 at St Cuthbert's Church as members of the United Associate Secession Congregation. George was 37 and his bride 24. George is described as an artist, living in 18 Bedford Street, Stockbridge, a suburb of Edinburgh. The couple moved to 7 Saunders Street, also in Stockbridge, and two years later their first child Thomas was born.

In 1832 the engraver James Johnstone made a proposal that was dear to George's heart, since it entailed making measurements and drawings of Scottish cathedrals and antiquities. It was intended to be a Scottish counterpart to *Cathedral Antiquities* by John Britton, an English antiquarian who was to become a friend of George. The project was taken over by Blackie and Son of Glasgow on the death of Johnstone in 1833 but, as so often was the case with George, the project never came to fruition. In 1834, at the expense of Blackie's, George focussed on Glasgow Cathedral, which he had already studied when he lived in that city earlier in his life. Glasgow Cathedral had suffered during the Reformation, like most ecclesiastical buildings in Scotland, and by the 19th century it was in a state of disrepair. An idea of restoration was conceived by Archibald McLellan, the Glaswegian coachbuilder and art connoisseur whose name is still commemorated in the McLellan Galleries in Sauchiehall Street, Glasgow, and in his collection of 400 paintings now in the Kelvingrove Museum. One of McLellan's proposals was to remove the Western Towers, thought by him, and many others at the time, to be out of keeping with the original medieval cathedral. A survey of the cathedral had been drawn up by the architect James Collie in 1835 and George was asked to produce some specific plans, which he duly did; these were lithographed and circulated at McLellan's expense. One of his drawings, of the proposed Western Tower restoration, is shown in Figure 20 (see page 56). He also illustrated his ideas, as was his practice, with a wooden model, which was completed later, in 1839.

It was in connection with this Glasgow Cathedral restoration project that George became embroiled in a controversy which, so his friends said later, affected him deeply. A local committee had been set up to oversee the repair project but despite the work that George had already put in, the very successful and prolific architect James Gillespie Graham was appointed to take the project forward, with McLellan's acquiescence and the approval of the Treasury (who were considering funding the restoration). Graham's plans, which were publicised by the committee, included George's drawings without acknowledgement to him. A rumour went around that George, through his drawings and model, was involved in some kind of 'spoiling' manoeuvre aimed at derailing Graham (despite the work being initiated well before Graham was involved). It took representations from his supporters and finally impassioned letters by George defending his position in 1840 to lay these rumours to rest. One of these letters was to McLellan, and is interesting in that it explains some of the decisions he took in relation to the design and demonstrates his in-depth knowledge of the dimensions of the cathedrals of England and Scotland.

20 George Meikle Kemp's restoration design for the Western Towers, Glasgow Cathedral. The design having been published by Archibald McLellan, Kemp's campaign to be acknowledged for his work failed when the established architect James Gillespie Graham took credit for it. Augustus Pugin also contributed a design but neither his nor Kemp's was adopted.

How did this all happen? The key point of this rather involved story (helpfully summarised in a 1997 article by James Macaulay for *The Architecture of Scottish Cities*) is that Graham, as an established architect, was able, and indeed thought it acceptable, to make use of drawings from many sources. Ironically, as Macaulay has shown, Graham was not even personally responsible for the final proposals for the Western Towers; rather it was the young English architect Augustus Pugin whose name may have been kept quiet in view of his conversion to Catholicism. In the end, none of these various plans came to anything due to lack of funding combined with an unfavourable opinion by Edward Blore, the architect of Buckingham Palace. The cathedral was eventually restored in the later 1840s, without the towers that had caused so much trouble.

One might speculate that there was some degree of 'ganging up' on the part of the architectural establishment. Architects had traditionally been trained as apprentices at an age of about 15 or 16, but in the 1830s and 1840s there was a move to include academic training, as described by David Walker[2] in his essay on the architectural profession in Scotland. The idea that only certain people could call themselves 'architects' as opposed to craftsmen, with an academic status on a par with lawyers or doctors, was taking hold. However, rather than being the victim of prejudice, an alternative explanation is that George simply did not have the right personality to fit into the accepted ways of commissioning public work. Whatever the reason for the unfortunate Glasgow Cathedral episode, it illustrates yet again George's knack of ending up on the wrong foot and somehow doing a great deal of work without much recognition.

Charles McKean, in the entry for George in the *Oxford Dictionary of National Biography*, asks a pertinent question: was he an 'architect' by this stage in his career, in the mid-30s? Evidence that he was not regarded by others as such comes from a speech made by his friend David Cousin. At a dinner held in honour of Bailie Dick, who had organised the financing of the completion of the Scott Monument, Cousin reported

2 www.scottisharchitects.org.uk

that the gossip around that time was that George 'had not even built a cow-house' (*The Scotsman*, 16 August 1851). Although unkindly put by the gossips, the accusation was probably true. While he had created theoretical reconstructions of Rosslyn Chapel, Trinity College Kirk, Melrose Abbey and Glasgow Cathedral, there is no evidence that he had produced designs for any new buildings.

Two churches, Millburn Church and Maybole West Church, have been attributed in the past to George but both were probably designed by others. Millburn Church, in Renton, West Dunbartonshire, is now believed to be designed by John Rochead in 1845, according to Historic Scotland (Listed Buildings, Ref: 1176) who note that George reputedly worked for a time at Millburn Tower. Perhaps this was the house built by William Atkinson at Ratho near Edinburgh in the early 19th century; there is also a Millburn House in Canaan Lane where George lived for a time. It has also been claimed that he designed Maybole West Church (Figure 21) between 1836 and 1840, possibly because of the second-hand

21 Maybole West Church. The design of this church has been attributed to George Meikle Kemp (dated between 1836 and 1840). Kemp did visit Ayrshire to make drawings of medieval buildings, but evidence from official documents relating to church affairs, combined with the date of building (1842), suggests that this church is unlikely to have been designed by him.

account in Bonnar that, in 1836, George was 'on his way to obtain the requisite data from which to prepare drawings for the Church of Maybole in Ayrshire'.

There is, however, evidence against the Maybole connection, in a report made by the Rev. George Gray to the Commissioners of Religious Instruction in Scotland (*House of Lords Sessional Papers*, 839, October 1838). He unequivocally stated that, in 1836, while the need for additional churches had been discussed at Maybole, no steps had been taken for their erection. Funding for a new church was only in place much later, in 1842. Furthermore, a report in *Chambers's Edinburgh Journal*, 21 April 1838, which seems to have been based on George's first- hand account, states that the journey was in fact to Kilwinning Abbey, Ayrshire, not to Maybole. George had also made drawings at Crossraguel Abbey ruins, two miles from Maybole: there is a drawing, untitled although clearly of Crossraguel, in the Kemp archive at the Writers' Museum. He may also have visited the Collegiate Church at Maybole, remains of which date from the 15th century. Architectural study of ancient buildings such as these would have been much more in line with his activities at that time than the design of a rather plain new church and would explain his visit to Ayrshire.

While there is little evidence for any productive architectural activity by George in the mid-1830s, it does seem that ideas about creative architecture – not just drawing existing buildings – may have been in George's mind from much earlier. His old apprentice master's son James Noble (*Berwickshire News*, 22 August 1871) recalled chatting with him in the early 1820s on the Calton Hill looking towards Princes Street, as in the view shown in Figure 22 (see page 60). In that conversation with his friend, George was dismissive of the buildings situated at that corner of Princes Street and told his friend that he dreamed of them being demolished and replaced by an impressive monument to a Scottish notable. However, the Glasgow Cathedral incident must have given him concerns about being taken seriously as an architect. Fortunately he had confidants in James Noble, and the Cousin family whom

22 *Edinburgh from Calton Hill* (by T. H. Shepherd, engraved by W. Tombleson, 1829). This view was the trigger for George Meikle Kemp's thoughts on the desirability of a monument to a national figure, which he expressed to his friend James Noble while chatting with him on Calton Hill.

whom he was close since his early days in their workshop. These people provided him with some solace in a period when he was trying to be regarded as more than just a draughtsman. Soon a chance to prove himself a bona fide architect – his heartfelt ambition – was about to present itself.

Chapter 5
The Scott Monument

On his way to Ayrshire in the spring of 1836, George called on a Glaswegian architect friend, a Mr Scott. His identity is not known for certain but he may have been Robert Scott, who had run an architectural academy in Glasgow since 1807 and who had designed, in 1825, one of the earliest Gothic revival churches in Scotland (St Mary's Episcopal Church in Renfield Street, Glasgow, now demolished). Scott showed George a newspaper advertisement for a competition to design a monument to Sir Walter Scott, who had died in 1832 and been buried in Dryburgh Abbey. The design was to include a statue and to cost less than £5,000 to construct; the three best designs would each receive a prize of 50 guineas. The competition would have been doubly attractive to George: not only did it offer a route into architecture but it would create a monument to a celebrated Scotsman, as he had envisaged when chatting to his friend on Calton Hill. He made a copy of the advertisement (a framing of which is held at the Writers' Museum) and resolved to enter the competition. He did so under the pseudonym of 'John Morvo' – the medieval mason of Melrose Abbey – and completed the design within five days. A transcript of a letter by him to his wife (*The Scotsman*, 29 August 1825), asking her to expedite the process of submitting the design via William Bonnar and David Cousin, shows how desperately keen he was to enter the competition.

The advertisement was not the beginning, nor indeed the end, of the search for a design for the monument, which was to take a further two years. A meeting had been called in 1832 by the Lord Provost of Edinburgh, John Learmonth, to consider a memorial to Sir Walter, and a committee of 'Noblemen and Gentlemen' was convened to organise the collection of subscriptions for the memorial. It was one of two committees set up to honour Sir Walter, the other being in London, but in the end the London Committee decided to use the money they had collected to pay off Scott's debts rather than contribute to a monument. The list of subscribers to the Edinburgh scheme, which comprised almost all of the great and good in Edinburgh at the time, was headed by the Bank of Scotland, which contributed £500.

The 'General Committee' subsequently set up a subcommittee (the 'Auxiliary Committee'), which was charged with deciding on the site for the monument, and its type. At this early stage the architectural artist David Roberts was invited to provide a design, which he did: two in fact, an Egyptian-style obelisk and a Gothic spire. These did not meet with approval from the subcommittee, and a number of other architects were approached. Two further designs then became available for consideration in 1835, an obelisk (see Figure 23) by William Henry Playfair, architect of the Royal Scottish Academy and the National Gallery of Scotland, and a Gothic spire by the English early Gothic revivalist Thomas Rickman. Again neither was judged adequate. It was then that a competition was proposed by the Duke of Buccleuch, and duly advertised in national newspapers. Fifty-four plans were submitted to the competition (22 Gothic structures, 11 statues, 14 Grecian temples, 5 pillars, one obelisk, and one fountain), and three winners were announced.

23 Proposed design for the Scott Monument by William Henry Playfair, 1835. A debate within the Monument Auxiliary Committee focussed on the choice between this classical type and a Gothic design. The latter was felt on balance to be more appropriate to Sir Walter Scott's memory.

On the day that the competition winners were announced, George was working at Linlithgow Palace taking drawings of a chimneypiece, unaware of the result of the competition. On returning to his home in Saunders Street, Stockbridge, he was told by his wife that the design of 'John Morvo' – George – was one of the three winning designs. The other two were by two eminent English architects, Charles Fowler along with the sculptor A.W. Leiver, and Thomas Rickman. The committee was still unconvinced by the three winning designs and solicited further entries, which included a resubmission by David Roberts, which again was not successful. Roberts implied later, in a letter to a friend, that his submissions were intended to 'give an idea to others' (perhaps suggesting that George might have used some of his ideas) and that his background stood against him. This may have been sour grapes, since he was reportedly upset at his rejection. George also submitted an improved version of his design, which certainly has some similarities with David Roberts' design (shown in Figure 24).

24 Proposed design for the Scott Monument by David Roberts, from 1834. Like George Meikle Kemp's design, it was in the Gothic style. After losing, Roberts said that the monument competition was a sore subject to him, although he later provided designs for the stained glass windows in the museum room in the monument.

Finally, on 28 March 1838, George was successful, his revised design (Figure 25, see page 66) winning the first of four prizes by a majority vote. All four prize-winning designs were in a Gothic style, which a majority of the subcommittee had decided would be consonant with Sir Walter's memory: it had been their stated preference even in 1834. It might seem that the Gothic faction had won the day over its rival group, the supporters of the classical obelisk.

The decision was not without controversy: Lord Meadowbank, especially, seemed to 'have it in' for the proposed design on grounds of its inappropriateness to the memory of Sir Walter. Robert Cadell, Scott's publisher, had initially favoured a Gothic design but later changed his mind and became a vociferous champion of the obelisk, perhaps under the influence of J.M.W. Turner (as Gerald Finley has argued in his 1980 study *Landscapes of Memory: Turner as Illustrator to Scott*). Cadell ridiculed the idea of the Gothic design and said that every retiring tradesman would build 'his pig styes with doors in imitation of those of a Gothic Cathedral'.

Cadell also protested about George's success, and even accused him of plagiarism. He called in aid the architect Thomas Hamilton, who claimed in a letter to *The Edinburgh Courant*, albeit in guarded terms, that George's design had similarities with some aspects of his own (unrealised) design for John Knox's church. Cadell then attempted to persuade the pro-obelisk faction to back him up in this charge. He made the accusations public in a pamphlet, and put in question George's qualification: it was he who made the comment that George 'had not built a cow house'. According to Bonnar, this pamphlet was sent (by chance) to be printed by a friend and relative of George's, who alerted him and thus gave him the chance to produce a counter-argument to be printed at the same time. George refuted the charge of plagiarism, and at the same time dealt with concerns about the stability of the structure voiced by Lord Meadowbank. Although rejecting Cadell's criticism of George's obscurity as an architect, Meadowbank nevertheless considered that the walls of his proposed monument would not 'stand one of our tempestuous winters'. George pointed out that rather than 'walls',

25 George Meikle Kemp's final competition drawing for the Scott Monument. He had been one of three prize winners in a competition to design a monument to Sir Walter Scott, but none was considered ideal by the judges. This was an improved version submitted to (and winning) the second stage in the competition.

the structure was made up of buttresses and piers which had an intrinsic strength.

The arguments within the subcommittee were described in the 1892 review of Bonnar's biography in *The Athenaeum* as 'pettifogging' and they took a long time to resolve. However, a day was fixed on which the committee was to make its final decision, and George was asked to attend the Royal Institution to explain the technicalities of his design. So much was riding on this discussion for his wife Elizabeth and her family that she appeared in person at the Royal Institution with her baby. Glimpsing her husband through the windows she tried to find out from him how his presentation was going, but was persuaded to wait in a local hotel, with a friend of George's relaying regular reports on progress. Finally the decision in favour of George's design was announced. As she said later, she handed George the baby and they walked back to their home in Stockbridge arm in arm, 'her happiness complete'. At last they would have a place in society and a regular income, and George could fulfill his creative ambitions.

William Burn was one of those in favour of George's submission and he had expressed his great admiration to the Committee of

> *...the elegance of Mr. Kemp's design, its purity as a Gothic composition, and more particularly the constructive skill exhibited throughout in the combination of the graceful features of that style of architecture, in such a manner as to satisfy any professional man of the correctness of its principle, and the perfect solidity which it would possess when built.*

While applauding the design, Burn was nonetheless keen to make sure that George did exactly what had been agreed to, and that he stayed within budget: he may have had some experience of trying to rein in George while he had been his employee. Although George refers to Burn respectfully in correspondence, he commented in a letter to his brother that he could be ruthless in using people to his own ends, and said that he would 'shift about like the cunning player at draughts.' He suspected Burn of trying to persuade him to accept a one-off fee and then to disappear from the scene, so it is clear that there was some degree of 'edge' in their mutual relations, despite Burn's favourable opinion of the design itself.

George's problems with Robert Cadell, William Burn and others are reminiscent of those he had faced in relation to the Glasgow Cathedral renovations, in that he had to fight his corner, supported by a loyal band of friends, against detractors. Some of the latter were no doubt sincere in their criticism, others perhaps motivated by professional jealousy. Whether he found himself in this position as a result of his rather quirky character – shy yet pugnacious – or merely through unfortunate circumstances is not always clear. Nevertheless, in the case of the Scott Monument he was on the winning side for the first time in his life.

The accepted design was initially not to George's proposed dimensions. Funds were only sufficient to build it to 135 feet (41 metres), not 184 feet (56 metres) as planned. He opposed the reduction in height, and wrote to his friend John Britton:

> *If the stairs are disagreeably narrow, the monument would lose half its interest to the citizens, and particularly to strangers. Enjoying a panoramic view of Edinburgh and the surrounding country from seventeen different galleries, at four easy stages from the ground, might create an excitement something like one of Scott's own romances.*

In this he was prescient: the climbing of the stairs and the view from the top is one of the main attractions of the monument in the present day. Joseph Woodfall Ebsworth drew four scenes from the top of the monument, facing towards all points of the compass, between 1845 and 1847. These pictures show a fascinating prospect of Edinburgh before some of the major changes to the streetscape with which we are now familiar, and one even shows an early example of a couple being photographed on a rooftop. Figure 26 shows one of these views; it must have been as stunning to Edinburgh citizens of the time as it is today. They are complemented by four modern day views by the Edinburgh artist Richard Demarco, created in 1986-87.

26 *View from the Scott Monument looking East*, 1847 (watercolour by Joseph Woodfall Ebsworth). Calton Hill, Arthur's Seat, and the original 1763 North Bridge connecting the Old and New Towns can be seen over the newly built railway. Ebsworth painted views facing four compass points (one of which shows the relatively new technology of photography in action, with a couple posing for a portrait on a rooftop).

The site was fixed in a central urban location, opposite the bottom of South St David Street in Princes Street, rather than in Charlotte Square, as had been initially proposed; various other sites had also been considered and rejected, including one opposite the West Bow, and others in Melville and Coates Crescents. Not all were pleased with this site at the time: an editorial in the *Caledonian Mercury*, 29 February 1840, considered that the choice of site could hardly be worse and would be a 'disgrace to the metropolis' since its view would be obscured by what they called incongruous sights, such as St Cuthbert's Church, Nelson's Monument and various dilapidated houses. David Lind was chosen as builder, out of a shortlist of five, much to George's satisfaction (his brother Thomas had dealt with him and also approved). The monument was to be of Binny sandstone from the shale beds at Linlithgow, West Lothian, a material popular for buildings in Edinburgh as it was readily carved, transportable via the Union Canal, and was durable and of a pleasant light-brown colour. Figure 27, a photograph by the pioneer photographers Robert Adamson and David Octavius Hill, shows the lightness of the original compared to the sooty colour of today – the disadvantage of this stone is that residual oil in it attracts soot, making it very difficult to clean, as later experience has shown.

27 An early photograph of the Scott Monument under construction in 1843 shortly before completion and before pollution darkened the stone. This is one of a series on the monument by the pioneer photographers Robert Adamson and David Octavius Hill, which they took from the top of the Royal Institution (now the Royal Scottish Academy building).

The original estimate for building the Scott Monument was £10,175, double the original sum specified in the competition, and it actually cost £16,154 to build (equivalent to over £700,000 today). The concerns about stability (valid, since tunnelling works were being carried out nearby by the Caledonian Railway Company) were mitigated by excavating the foundations 52 feet (16 metres) into bedrock – this added to the cost. The extra money was gathered through subscriptions, which arrived from as far afield as St Petersburg, and the available funds were further increased through the exertions of two enterprising Princes Street residents. As described in the report of the foundation ceremony in *The Scotsman*, 19 August 1840, they divided the city into 100 districts and, with their friends, personally lay in wait for inhabitants until they handed over some cash. They even managed to extract a total of over £3 from 40 of the 'humblest ranks' of the Cowgate, as the paper describes them.

John Steell was chosen to make the sculpture of Scott for the base of the monument. He was then a relatively unknown sculptor but was knighted in 1876 and appointed as Sculptor to Queen Victoria (see Rocco Lieuallen's 2002 academic biography for more information on Steell). Although the choice of sculptor was unanimous among those who voted, Robert Cadell again went against the tide in favouring the English sculptor Francis Chantrey who had made a much-admired bust of Sir Walter in 1820. While Chantrey did not get the commission, Steell was invited to use his bust as a model. Steell later created a number of sculptures around Edinburgh, and statues of Robert Burns and Sir Walter Scott for New York City (the latter a copy of the Edinburgh statue).

The marble for the statue (the first outdoor statue made of such material in Scotland) was imported from Italy. It was so heavy that it fell through the ship into Livorno harbour; it then required twenty horses to transport it from Leith docks to Steell's studio, the weight of the carriage cutting grooves into the streets. Figure 28 (see page 72) shows the statue. Twice life-size, it was completed in 1846, and depicts Sir Walter and one of his dogs (said to be his favourite, Maida, although possibly modelled from another dog since Maida had died by then). He is shown in naturalistic pose, with a book reflecting his calling as writer, and he is dressed in a shepherd's plaid which makes reference to his rural background but also gives him an outline of classical seriousness.

George was suspicious of Robert Cadell's motives in relation to the sculpture, perhaps not surprisingly given his ruthlessness, and wrote to his brother Thomas that Cadell had tried to organise forces against him, and that he was trying to 'get money into the hands of Chantry [sic]'. This interpretation of events may have been an example of George's obsession with the malign influence of money on others, which he had expressed on a number of occasions in letters. By contrast, he seems to have been genuinely unconcerned with his own

28 John Steell's sculpture of Sir Walter Scott (1846), photographed at night. The sculpture is twice life size, and was the first outdoor statue of Carrara marble to be made in Scotland. The (male) deerhound Maida in the sculpture was Scott's favourite and was also the subject of a painting by Alexander Nasmyth.

financial situation, at least according to a story by Bonnar. Despite the generous prize in the initial stage of the competition (about £3,000 today), George mislaid the original prize cheque until some months later, having cleared it away with his usual absent-mindedness when a visitor appeared at the door.

In March 1840 George invited friends to witness what he called the real (as opposed to the ceremonial) foundation on the bedrock and, in the depths of the earth, he invited them to drink a toast. His friends included the builder David Lind, the sculptor Alexander Handyside Ritchie (who was to sculpt a bust of George, shown on the front cover), and artist and writer James Ballantine. He painted the stained glass windows for the monument inserted in the museum room on the first floor in 1854. These had been designed by David Roberts, one of the original competitors. Windows by Ballantine can be seen today in the restaurant of the Café Royal in Edinburgh, and there are also examples in St Giles' Cathedral.

In May 1840 the subcommittee decided that the design should be fully carried out to George's original dimensions and the official laying of the foundation stone was carried out that year, on 15 August, Sir Walter Scott's birthday. The ceremony was conducted by Sir James Forrest, Lord Provost of the City of Edinburgh and Grand Master Mason of Scotland. The foundation stone contained a plate with an inscription to the memory of Sir Walter by Lord Jeffrey, and another contributed by the Grand Lodge of Scotland. An unusually early example of a time capsule was deposited, in the form of a glass jar containing newspapers, copies of inscription plates, a plan of Edinburgh, a list of subscribers, a number of coins, and a medal struck for the occasion. A silver trowel used for the ceremony was presented to Sir James by the Lodge of Edinburgh, No. 1 (Mary's Chapel). A speech by Sir William Rae and a seven-gun salute concluded the ceremony. The assembled crowds no doubt appreciated the efforts of the Edinburgh Tee-total Band as they drowned out the prayer and the Lord Provost's address, despite attempts to quell them (*The Scotsman*, 19 August 1840).

29 Masons working on a gryphon during the construction of the Scott Monument, photographed by Robert Adamson and David Octavius Hill in about 1844. The masons are working in a builders' hut similar to that in Nasmyth's painting (Figure 13, on page 39). Many would have succumbed to 'stone-cutters' disease' after inhaling the dust, as the geologist and essayist Hugh Miller, himself a mason, had written.

The success of the day was primarily due to the enormous regard in which Sir Walter Scott was held. It is hard to get to grips with the extent of this, especially as his works are far less popular nowadays compared to then. He was regarded as almost on a par with Shakespeare, not just in Scotland, but also in Europe and America, as Stuart Kelly has described in *Scott-land: The Man Who Invented a Nation*. It was only because of this public adulation that a monument of such a scale could have been financed: it was (and is) the largest to an author in the world. The celebrity of Sir Walter drew the crowds to the foundation ceremony, and of course many would have jumped at the chance for what was, in those days, an all-too-rare public holiday. George was able to enjoy a day of triumph as one of the central figures in this great event.

In order for the monument to proceed, an Act of Consent was required from Parliament to overturn a prohibition against building on the south side of Princes Street; this was granted in 1841. George took on the role of Clerk of Works himself, rather than hand over day-to-day management of the monument project. According to the catalogue of the Scott Centenary Exhibition in 1871 (which drew together memorabilia connected with Scott, including some concerning the monument) a model of the monument was exhibited in Princes Street, and was visited by Queen Victoria. It is now held in the Museum Collections Centre in Edinburgh (and a similar one is displayed in the Writers' Museum). Some of the masons, who would have worked from the model as well as from the plans, appear in a number of photographs by Adamson and Hill (a group working on a gryphon during the construction of the Scott Monument is shown in Figure 29).

With a loyal band of masons under his supervision, and some degree of financial security, all seemed set fair for George's future as architect and respected member of Edinburgh society, and work on the monument began in earnest in 1841.

Chapter 6
Final Years in Edinburgh

The job of Clerk of Works was to provide a useful source of income for George. As well as the financial benefit of taking on the project management, there was also the important psychological bonus that he could oversee and control his masterwork. The building of the Scott Monument proceeded without major incident. It is likely that many of the masons would have succumbed to silicosis – the 'stonecutter's disease', as described by Hugh Miller, himself originally a mason. Nevertheless a report on the inauguration ceremony (*The Scotsman*, 19 April 1846) noted that there had been no accidents during the construction. This was an unusual occurrence for major works in that time (and indeed in our time). The photograph by Adamson and Hill (Figure 30) shows George taking a rest on the building site, where he would have been visible almost daily to passers-by on Princes Street; this constant presence probably contributed to his immense public popularity in Edinburgh. He is shown in his characteristic thoughtful pose, with his bouffant hairstyle and clothes covered in dust.

30 George Meikle Kemp, photographed by Robert Adamson and David Octavius Hill in about 1843. He holds plans for the construction of the Scott Monument; calipers, a tool box, and a T-square can be seen. His bouffant hairstyle and clothes are covered in dust and he has a thoughtful expression, also evident in the bust of him by Alexander Handyside Ritchie.

Despite the public acclaim, new sources of income for George were few and far between. As he remarked in a letter to his brother Thomas:

> *Trade is very dull here, particularly in the building line: with the exception of some shop-fronts, and some talk of a cheap kirk or two, I hear of nothing else.*

At one stage George hoped that he might form a partnership with his brother to bid for other schemes. The Glasgow Cathedral renovation project, for example, would have made a useful complement to the Scott Monument work. George entertained hopes for this; a cousin, Joseph Mowbray, was still helping him with a model of the cathedral, as well as the model of the Scott Monument. However, although his Glasgow Cathedral drawings had been published by Archibald McLellan, his plans for its renovation were not realised (see Chapter 4). The drawings showed off George's skill as an architectural artist, so the proposed book on ecclesiastical buildings and antiquities would have been anticipated with interest: the article about George in *Chambers's Edinburgh Journal*, 21 April 1838 noted that the book's sponsor, James Johnstone, had died, and expressed hope that the project would be fulfilled, albeit after 'an elapse of time'. Perhaps with this in mind, George continued, at least for a time, to make trips to Melrose, Jedburgh and Kelso abbeys. Despite the interest in the press about the project, the antiquities book never appeared.

A question arises as to how far George may have got with the book and whether he had considered a potential career in illustration, in addition to his architectural ambitions. There are some preliminary sketches of buildings from various parts of Scotland in the Writers' Museum archive. A few completed drawings, such as those of Glasgow Cathedral and of Melrose Abbey, were engraved and appeared as illustrations in compilations of Scottish topography, both contemporary and some published in the latter half of the 19th century. These early drawings appeared in 1833 in proofs of a magazine, *The Republic of Letters* (edited by Alexander Whitelaw). There were also a few later drawings of sites in Edinburgh, including one of St Giles' Cathedral shown in

Figure 31, made after 1835 as it depicts a well which was constructed only then. George also drew, in addition, various views from Salisbury Crags over to Calton Hill, including his reconstruction of the National Monument; these date from after the Scott Monument competition.

31 *View of St Giles, Edinburgh, from West* (engraving by Thomas Dick for *Scotland Illustrated*, 1845, after George Meikle Kemp). One of several drawings Kemp made of places in Edinburgh which appeared in various compendium books on Scottish topography, but which were never gathered together in one place (despite early plans for a book of such drawings).

As noted above, some of George's drawings appear as single items in various books, but there seems to be no corpus of finished pieces that might have gone into the proposed book on antiquities. There are no records of any formal agreements regarding the publication of this book in the Blackie's archives held by the University of Glasgow. Quite the reverse in fact, as the records show that George owed the company

£8/16/9d for posting bills, relating to his claim to be responsible for the redesign of the Western Towers of Glasgow Cathedral, and for circular letters, probably on the same topic. The sums owed were dated between 1839 and 1840, and were set off as a bad debt in June 1843. There is no evidence of any agreement to produce further drawings and had there been any fees, these would surely have been set against the outstanding debt.

Given that the accounts record is the last evidence of any connection with Blackie's, one has to assume that George did not pursue the book project for very long, perhaps not surprisingly given that monument duties would have taken up most of his time. The fact that *Chambers's Edinburgh Journal* refers in 1838 to the need for further time before the book's publication, even five years after the publisher Johnstone's death, implies that George had not made much progress and the article may have been reflecting wishful thinking or at least over-optimism on his part. After George's death, William Burn (who had already been planning for this) subsidised the English architect Robert William Billings to illustrate a four-volume publication along the same lines, *The Baronial and Ecclesiastical Antiquities of Scotland*. This work, published between 1845 and 1852, was to become a classic on the subject, and has recently been republished.

George has been described by Julian Halsby and Paul Harris in The Dictionary of Scottish Painters as a watercolour artist, working in the style of Thomas Hamilton. However, examples by him in this medium are difficult to identify. The National Galleries of Scotland hold a watercolour of the Royal Institution, now the Royal Scottish Academy, dated to about 1840, which shows George's fine draughtsmanship (Figure 32, see page 82). An engraving by W. Deeble of the same scene, dated 1839, was found at the back of the watercolour on its acquisition, and an earlier version of this engraving dating from 1837 is held by the Edinburgh Central Library. This earlier date implies that, if the engraving was taken directly from the watercolour (and the colour was not added later) the watercolour must date to 1837 (it cannot be earlier since John Steell's sphinxes, added in that year, are evident).

32 *The Royal Institution, Edinburgh* (watercolour by George Meikle Kemp). The Royal Institution was where the deliberations of the Scott Monument Committee took place, and where Kemp's son Thomas was educated (at Board of Manufactures' design courses). An engraving of the same scene was found at the back of this drawing. The building now houses the Royal Scottish Academy.

Of course the colour in the Royal Institution watercolour may have been added later, as was commonly done in that period. This almost certainly happened with other of his works. We might take as examples two coloured images of West Bow in Edinburgh in the collections of the National Galleries of Scotland, apparently by George and his brother-in-law William Bonnar as joint creators. They are described as being in gouache but as late as 1860, and hence after George's death, two of these drawings were described by J.A. Wylie as being 'original drawings in India ink'. A reasonable inference is that the professional painter Bonnar coloured George's drawings after his death. A third coloured drawing in the Galleries attributed to George, of Heriot's Hospital and the Grassmarket, appeared in *Scotland Illustrated* of 1850 and is described there as 'drawn and engraved by T. Dick'. Two works in the same volume, of the National Monument and of Arthur's Seat, have George's name specifically attached as artist (like the other artists used in the publication) so perhaps it can be inferred that the Heriot's Hospital engraving was in fact by T. Dick, as stated on the illustration. Thus, while George produced several fine pen-and-ink drawings, evidence for his work as a watercolourist is thin.

Finally on the topic of George's artistic creations, although probably from much earlier, there is an interesting portrait of James Moir attributed to him, in the Scottish National Portrait Gallery. The portrait was donated in 1938 by Moir's descendants who stated that it had been given by George to Moir, a fellow wright and lodger (there was certainly a James Moir, a wright, who lived in Stockbridge in 1829 around the time George lived in that area). Notes of correspondence with a Keeper at the Scottish National Portrait Gallery show that he had considered an intriguing possibility: that, rather than being a portrait of Moir, it was in fact a self-portrait in view of its similarity to George's known likenesses. Figure 33 shows this portrait next to one of George by Bonnar, and indeed the resemblance is striking. A further piece of evidence

33 (a) Detail from portrait of George Meikle Kemp by William Bonnar (b) *James Moir, fl. c. 1830*, attributed to George Meikle Kemp. James Moir was a fellow-craftsman friend and co-lodger. The idea that (b) may in fact have been a self-portrait by Kemp has been mooted, because of the resemblance to his known likenesses, such as that shown in (a), and the right-to-left buttoning of his waistcoat.

is the waistcoat, buttoning right-over-left in (b) and so contrary to conventional gentleman's dress. This suggests a mirror-image, a marker of a self-portrait. If George did create this portrait (whether of himself or of Moir) it would be unusual, as the subject matter of his drawings was otherwise entirely architectural. If it is a self-portrait it would be even more interesting as it would depict George as a young man, possibly before he married.

Despite his somewhat precarious financial position, which depended almost entirely on the Scott Monument, George was by all accounts contented. After moving from Stockbridge to 5 Canning Place, Causewayside, by May 1838 he had moved to Bloomberry Cottage (at the junction of Newbattle Terrace and Canaan Lane in Morningside), in the then rural area of Canaan. He stayed there for a year, and was very happy with the move: he and Elizabeth had a garden stocked with fruit and vegetables, and the property was economical to run. George had become a family man; his eldest son Thomas had been born in 1833 and his daughters Elizabeth and Jane were born in 1837 and 1838 respectively. In 1841 his second son William George was born. Although William was to become a professional artist, it was his first son Thomas who was the chip off the old block. He is shown in Figure 34 in a drawing by an Italian artist Felice Pitconie. This was the friend who had been scrumping for apples with George during his travelling days, and who had later visited him in Edinburgh. Little is known about this artist, although he was engaged in helping to make the bust of the Duke of Sutherland on his death in 1833 (probably assisting Francis Chantrey).

Thomas was a budding architect, and became apprenticed to George's friend David Cousin, studying at the Board of Manufactures' Drawing Academy (this was situated at the Royal Institution building and was ultimately to lead to the Edinburgh College of Art). Thomas continued his father's interest in Rosslyn, exhibited a number of drawings of the inside of the chapel, and had ideas of his own for its reconstruction and that of Roslin castle. He would have been a great source of pride to his parents, but George was to die before he was able to see Thomas

34 *Thomas Kemp* (by Felice Pitconie). The Italian artist Felice Pitconie met George Meikle Kemp while they were both travelling in France and later came to work in Scotland, visiting Kemp in Edinburgh. Thomas, Kemp's eldest son, was talented and had hoped to become an architect like his father, but he was a sickly youth and died shortly after his return from a study tour of the Continent.

awarded a Royal Scottish Academy travelling prize. Sadly, Thomas died aged about twenty in December 1853 following his return from a study tour on the Continent. The cause of his death is not known but he was a sickly young man whose mother was constantly urging him in letters to look after himself and eat properly.

George had been described in *The Post-Office Annual Directory for 1838-9* when at Bloomberry Cottage, Canaan Lane as 'artist', but he appears as 'architect' in the directories for 1839-40 when residing at 25 Parkside Street near Holyrood Park, and a year later at 33 Parkside Street (in the 1843-44 directories, he is listed at Jordan Lane, Morningside). By 1839 he thus considered himself primarily as an architect: concerned with the structure and not just the appearance of buildings. He was also becoming known by others as an expert on medieval architecture. In 1837 George had revisited his old stamping ground of Rosslyn Chapel, and exhibited a drawing of its interior at the Scottish Academy.

The chapel was a source of controversy among the major architects and antiquarians of the time. This was partly fuelled by Sir Walter Scott's revival of the legend of the burial there of the fully-armed bodies of ten barons of the Sinclair family, referred to in *The Lay of the Last Minstrel*. More seriously, there were fundamentally differing approaches within the architectural profession about the merits of conservation versus restoration or even redesign, an account of which has been given by Angelo Maggi. George had a peripheral role in this argument: in 1840, at the request of the English architect John Britton, he reported on the method of construction of the side aisles of the chapel and on the progress of William Burn's reconstruction work there. George would have been gratified had he known that Britton was to quote from his notes in a lecture on the chapel and its restoration to the Royal Institute of British Architects in 1846.

George was, by the 1840s, a respected member of Edinburgh society. The portrait (Figure 35) by his brother-in-law, William Bonnar, from about 1840, shows him in this persona with the unfinished monument in the background. A song, 'The Gem o' Edina', was dedicated to him by Alex McLaggan and published in *The Scotsman*, 25 November 1843. Each of the five verses ends with a couplet such as this:

Then hurrah for the beauty and grandeur that's blent
In the gem o' Edina – The Scott Monument!

This public acknowledgement of his almost-completed creation would have been immensely encouraging to George, given his early struggles.

One mark of George's integration into Edinburgh society was the appearance of one of his little songs, 'O come awa, Jeannie', in David Robertson's 1842 song book *Whistle-binkie* (a Scots word meaning a person attending a wedding who was fed free in return for entertainment; see Figure 36 on page 88). This song was set to music by Peter McLeod, a printer and well-known amateur composer who produced compilations such as *Original National Melodies of Scotland* and *New National Songs*. The latter contains several songs by James Ballantine – the same Ballantine who had made the stained-glass windows for the monument. George's song contains advice to a daughter, the import of which was that fine folks such as the laird's son were likely to be unreliable

35 *George Meikle Kemp, 1795 - 1844. Architect and designer of the Scott Monument* (oil on panel, by William Bonnar, about 1840), given to the National Gallery of Scotland by Thomas Bonnar (Kemp's nephew by marriage and his biographer). The partially-built Scott Monument can just be seen in the background.

and that she should rather encourage as a suitor 'Hughy Graham o' the Windlestrae dell', who was 'guileless like herself'. Although the music used for his song is not printed with the words, they fit a number of melodies with a jig metre that McLeod provided for Ballantine's songs, including 'What ails my minnie at Willie and me' ('minnie' being a Scots word meaning mother) which had subject matter somewhat similar to that of 'O come awa, Jeannie'.

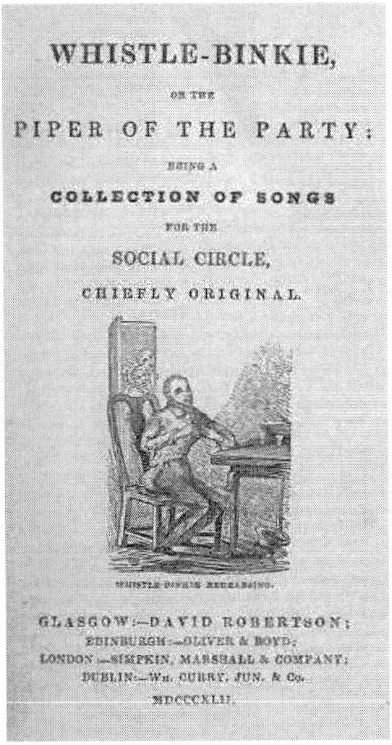
WHISTLE-BINKIE,
OR THE
PIPER OF THE PARTY:
BEING A
COLLECTION OF SONGS
FOR THE
SOCIAL CIRCLE,
CHIEFLY ORIGINAL.

GLASGOW:—DAVID ROBERTSON;
EDINBURGH:—OLIVER & BOYD;
LONDON:—SIMPKIN, MARSHALL & COMPANY;
DUBLIN:—WM. CURRY, JUN. & CO.
MDCCCXLII.

36 Title page of David Robertson's 1842 song book, *Whistle-binkie or the Piper of the Party*. A 'whistle-binkie' was someone invited to eat and drink at weddings in exchange for entertainment. This pocket-sized book contained contributions from known and unknown poets of the time, often in Scots, and included 'O Come Awa, Jeannie', one of many poems composed by George Meikle Kemp.

Whistle-binkie was issued in five series from 1832. It was of a size to fit in the pocket and contained poems and songs by well-known writers as well as by amateur gentlemen (and the occasional lady). They vied to have their creations included, sending in unsolicited contributions, too many to publish. The editor was relentlessly upbeat, insisting that 'no atrabilarious [characterised by melancholy] effusion has been permitted to stain our pages', and the volume was filled with material to brighten up social gatherings. George was known to pull out his violin on such occasions and to give renditions of comic songs and verse that he knew by heart. It seems that despite his shyness he was good company among those he knew, as his obituary later made clear:

> *His habits of solitary meditation prevented him from expressing his thoughts readily to strangers, but to a numerous circle of friends he was at all times an instructive and delightful companion.*

According to Bonnar, George also actively participated in debating – an activity that was widespread at all levels of society in Edinburgh from the Enlightenment onwards. For those of lowly backgrounds it could provide a means of self-education: James Hogg (the Scottish poet and novelist also known as the Ettrick Shepherd) tells of how, in his youth in the countryside, he and fellow shepherds would meet to discuss essays on prearranged topics. Organised debating clubs in the city ranged from the serious (such as the exclusive Speculative Society whose members were chosen by ballot) to more socially open societies, such as the Forum, of which James Hogg became secretary (see Gillian Hughes' article on this subject). This was the type of club that George may have attended. However, the essays which Bonnar attributed to George are in a somewhat different handwriting to George's usual, and are clearly the work of one of the office bearers. Acting as an office bearer was hardly an activity that George would have relished, given his retiring nature. Furthermore, he did not seem to be particularly interested in general ethical or political debate. Despite having travelled in Glasgow, Lancashire and France in the early years of the century, his letters make no mention of social upheavals and political activity in these places, other than to comment adversely on what he saw as the particular social habits of the upper classes. He was much more concerned with aesthetic matters such as literature and architecture, and his own visionary speculations.

Apart from the Scott Monument, examples of George's architecture from this period are hard to find. He made plans for widening the North Bridge (*The Scotsman*, 9 March 1842) but these were not taken up by the Edinburgh Town Council, and the bridge was not widened until 1874 (and dismantled for renewal in 1896). He also designed a plinth for Sueno's Stone, an ancient Pictish monument in Forres on the Moray coast. It turned out, however, that the stone could not be moved without permission of its then owner, the Earl of Moray, and since this was not forthcoming there was no question of moving it onto a new plinth (*Caledonian Mercury*, 3 July 1842). In 1843, presumably because he foresaw the Scott Monument income coming to an end, he took on work on a new wing at Woodhouselee, Glencorse, Midlothian for James Tytler the Third, fees for which were still owing to him on his death. The house has been demolished, but the stables are now in use as a private residence, and according to Historic Scotland these may have been built by George.

In the early part of 1844 public excitement must have been growing, as the great edifice of the Scott Monument neared completion. Its gradual growth from foundations deep in the ground to the soaring peak of its delicate pinnacle was a daily spectacle, and progress could be judged against the wooden model which guided the masons. The public must also have anticipated future novel and beautiful buildings to be designed by George, once he could be freed from the arduous job of overseeing the building of the monument. Indeed, *The Edinburgh Post* (cited by *The Glasgow Herald*, 25 March 1844) claimed that 'several lucrative commissions had begun to flow upon him' around this time. No doubt these would have been in the back of George's mind as he set off for home after he had spent an evening, one Wednesday in March, with his builder David Lind in South Charlotte Street. His wife Elizabeth would have eagerly awaited him that night, perhaps speculating about the next phase of his career in a few months' time, after the completion of the monument. But she was never to see him again. Her hopes for George's career and for his proper recognition after many years of struggle came to nothing. George failed to return home: he had met an untimely – and still unexplained – death.

Walking back home on that foggy evening of 6 March 1844, George had seemingly crossed the Union Canal at Fountainbridge rather than at Semple Street, which would have been his usual route home. His walking stick, a present from his brother-in-law, was found and his body was recovered from the canal near the Lochrin Distillery the following Monday, identified by his hat which was attached to his coat and found floating in the canal. *The Scotsman*, 20 March 1844, reported his death as a melancholy accident, but was his death suicide, murder or tragic misadventure? George had, by all accounts, a happy family and social life, and his extraordinarily positive attitude to life's setbacks would argue against suicide. Murder by a rival is even more unlikely: although some of his fellow architects may have resented his good fortune in winning the Scott Monument competition he was no real competitor to any, not having an established business that might have diminished any of their own commercial opportunities.

Hugh Miller, in his article in *The Witness*, 'The Late Mr Kemp', described the scene of his death:

> *A high wall, perforated by a low, clumsy archway, closes abruptly what the stranger might deem a thoroughfare. There is a piece of sluggish, stagnant water on the one hand, thick and turbid, and somewhat resembling in form and colour a broad muddy highway, lined by low walls; not a tuft of vegetation is to be seen on its tame rectilinear sides: all is slimy and brown, with here and there dank, muddy recesses, as if for the frog and the rat.*

Figure 37 shows a photograph of the wooden bridge over the canal at Semple Street as it was in the early 20th century before it was redeveloped, a gloomy place even then.

37 The wooden bridge over the Union Canal at Semple Street, Fountainbridge, Edinburgh, photographed in about 1900. This was where George Meikle Kemp would normally cross on his way home after visiting his builder. Kemp's body was found in the canal near the Lochrin Distillery on the foggy night of 6 March 1844. Reports suggest that he fell from the towpath, having missed the turning. The circumstances of his death have not been entirely explained.

John Bonnar (George's nephew and brother of his biographer) said that George had been found at the 'toom' on the East side of the canal, not near the towpath, and at a place which was surrounded by a parapet 4-5 feet (1-1.5 metres) high. This was where dustcarts emptied their loads into the canal ('toom' is a Scots word for 'to empty'), so the water would have been particularly turbid from their murky overspill. George was reputedly a strong swimmer but would have had particular problems here. This location is somewhat mysterious: there is no obvious explanation of what he was doing there, unless he had been thrown over the parapet by footpads targeting a lone walker in the fog. There certainly were several court cases in Edinburgh during 1843-44 involving boatmen and others stealing from boats or assaulting people near the canal. Indeed, on receiving the walking stick as a gift from his brother-in-law, George had said, according to Bonnar:

> *This will be a grand thing for effectually keeping off the roughs who infest that part of the Canal banks after nightfall.*

By a strange coincidence, a few weeks after George's death one Arthur Hart, an illiterate carter who had criminal form, was convicted in the High Court and transported to Tasmania for seven years. He had been stealing from a boat containing goods belonging to David Lind (George's builder), which was moored near the spot where George's body was found. Did George call in at the boat to look at the stones that were to be used for the monument? Might he have disturbed Hart or one of his criminal associates in this insalubrious area and met his death as a result?

One theory was (and in some quarters still is) that he 'had drink taken' and had fallen into the canal as a result. This last theory is discounted as ridiculous by Bonnar, although he admitted that the story was current even among some who knew George personally. The very fact that Bonnar felt he had to mention it (given his usual adulatory approach) suggests that it may have been a case of 'no smoke without fire'. Just after his death, Lord Cockburn said that George was 'drunk as usual' in a letter to Lord Jeffrey. Certainly George was hardly a teetotaler. He bemoaned the absence of a glass of Glenlivet in a letter from London and he regaled his friends with a drink in the vaults underneath the monument. On a foggy night, someone with one or two drams inside them could easily become disorientated and perhaps prey to robbers.

The announcement of his death caused an outpouring of public grief, as shown by the huge crowds who were to attend the funeral, and by the financial aid gathered to help his bereaved family, including funds raised through a benefit concert. The arrangements for the funeral were, however, contentious. It was mooted by some members of the committee that George should be buried underneath the monument, although Lord Cockburn for one strongly objected. He disliked the monument (although he later recanted, perhaps realising the benefits to tourism). In view of this and his remarks on George's lack of sobriety, he seems not to have been well-disposed to him and in a letter addressed to Sir Thomas Dick-Lauder he said that the monument had been built to memorialise Scott and no one else. Despite this objection, the funeral papers did in fact state that the grave should be under the Scott Monument, according to Hugh Miller. However, to the consternation of the onlookers the funeral procession was delayed by an hour and had to change course at the last minute, perhaps at the request of the family. According to Bonnar the idea was considered by the family as being inappropriate; George's other nephew John Bonnar also stated that it had been 'busybodies' who had suggested the idea.

The starting point for the procession was, according to Miller, a cottage in Morningside. It has been suggested that George had returned to his previous home at Bloomberry Cottage in 1843 (letter, *The Scotsman*, 18 May 1932) but the more probable venue is one of the cottages in Jordan Lane, George's last listing in the Post-Office Directory. The final destination was the graveyard of St Cuthbert's (then known as the West Church, and mostly rebuilt in 1893). Figure 38 shows the gravestone which was to mark the resting place for George and his family. The masons who had worked for him carried the coffin, which was accompanied by members of the Royal Scottish Academy, the Scott Monument Committee and members and representatives of various public bodies. The crowds that attended the procession were a testament to George's popularity, which was to last many years after his death, and reverberates even today.

38 The Kemp family gravestone at St Cuthbert's Church at the West End of Edinburgh. There had been a proposal to bury George Meikle Kemp under the Scott Monument but the site was changed at the last minute. The tombstone includes a medallion portrait by Alexander Handyside Ritchie, who also made a bust of Kemp.

Chapter 7

George Meikle Kemp's Legacy

Following George's tragic death, Hugh Miller observed that

> *...the poor deceased..., though he had risen, after a long struggle, into celebrity, had not risen into affluence.*

He also commented on the humble appearance of the house from which the burial cortège left. Indeed, the family was in some hardship. George left his wife Elizabeth (shown in Figure 39) only £202, some furniture, and a model of Glasgow Cathedral, very little for her to live on. She lived to be 81 years old and died in Newington, Edinburgh in 1889.

39 Mrs Elizabeth Kemp, George Meikle Kemp's widow (and sister of William Bonnar). This photograph may have been taken by her son-in-law Robert Kemp Thomson, a professional photographer who moved from Edinburgh to Wigtown, Dumfries and Galloway. She provided her nephew Thomas Bonnar with material for his biography of Kemp.

Elizabeth Kemp had to take work as a seamstress, as did her daughter Elizabeth. Records suggest that her other daughter Jane may have attended John Watson's Institution, founded in 1828 for destitute Scottish children, most of whom had lost at least one parent (she qualified for entry as a fatherless child). Jane's middle name is given as Meikle or Mowbray; the former is on the gravestone but the latter appears on the death certificate (registered by a neighbour). Of George's other children, William may have attended Donaldson's Hospital, the school for the deaf, which had a link with George's maternal ancestors the Braidwoods. (There is no evidence that he was actually deaf; the school also took some hearing children.) These attendances would have been charitably funded, and one might wonder why the Bonnars, who were a substantial family, were not more evident in support of the Kemps. However, two Bonnar family members, Wilhelmina and Ann, lived with the Kemps at various times, so there may have been an unrecorded financial arrangement. In any case the public rallied round with a memorial concert to support the family and the Freemasons also contributed. Subscriptions were gathered for George's son Thomas to study architecture in Italy, including one from the Duke of Buccleuch's estate.

George's son William made a living first as an engraver and then as a landscape painter. By the time of the 1881 census, his mother and his sister Jane were living with him. William married Elizabeth Storrie in 1902; after his death in 1904 his widow married the jeweller Peter Westren. As Mrs Kemp-Westren she donated a painting of George to the Edinburgh City Council and after her death her sister Mrs Tait donated a bureau-bookcase made by George to the Writers' Museum. George's daughter Elizabeth married an Edinburgh accountant, Robert Thomson, whose son Robert Kemp Thomson became an 'artist and photographer' based initially in Edinburgh and latterly in Wigtown, Dumfries and Galloway. He married twice, to Jane Ross and Helen Forbes, and these Thomson families seem to be George's only identifiable direct descendants, as Jane and William had no recorded offspring.

Of George's siblings, Thomas died in 1841 in Dalkeith leaving a daughter Helen, who was single when she died. She was a governess in Joppa where she seems to be remembered for general cantankerousness. She is said to have owned the Kemp family Bible, but its whereabouts are now unknown. Jane (or Jean) married James Johnstone, a farm worker; she died in Humbie, East Lothian in 1878. George's tool chest is reputed to have been in the possession of her grandson John Tait, stationmaster at Nisbet Station near Jedburgh. Janet married John Anderson, a shepherd, and died in Gladsmuir, East Lothian in 1877. Isobel married Alexander Downs, an ostler (having run off with him during the reading of the banns for another man to whom she was engaged). She died in 1870 in Edinburgh. Violet, the youngest sister, married a ploughman, who was latterly an estate factor and expert in cattle breeding at Kilmory, Argyll. She died in Glasgow in 1889; among her descendants is the celebrated Scottish artist Dame Elizabeth Violet Blackadder. The Adamson and Hill photograph of a Miss Kemp, sometimes identified as George's sister, for example in the catalogue of the National Portrait Gallery in London, Ref: NPG P6(121), is now thought to be a member of a completely different Kemp family (see Photograph Group 150 in Sara Stevenson's Adamson-Hill catalogue).

George's death caused consternation in the Scott Monument Committee, although they were relieved that his brother-in-law William Bonnar offered to take over management of the monument for no fee, and that he stated that he would follow George's design without deviation, although in fact he increased the height by about 25 feet (about 8 metres) more than that specified in the original design. Whether or not the increase was in line with George's intentions is not known but it added to the expense. According to Bonnar, the workmen offered to work for nothing for two weeks to meet this, although their contribution was not necessary in the end, as funds were obtained from subscriptions.

One of George's own ideas, to create a decorative screen at the base of the monument with Gothic towers in the corners and white marble steps, was not carried out and the monument was left with its plain and somewhat forbidding steps. Just a few days before George's death, a landscape gardener, Craigie Halkett, was invited by the Monument Committee to lecture on the development of the surroundings. He presented the idea of a raised esplanade around the monument, with an ornamental wall and lines of poplars (*Caledonian Mercury*, 4 March 1844). This never happened and the monument was completed in the autumn of 1844, with George's ten-year-old son Thomas placing the capstone.

A drawing (Figure 40) shows the crowds who attended the inauguration ceremony in 1846. The Edinburgh merchants and the Freemasons, who had taken the major part in ensuring the completion of the monument, were well represented at the event which, like the foundation ceremony, was accompanied by some pomp.

40 A drawing, by an unknown artist, of the inauguration ceremony for the Scott Monument held on 15 August 1846. Following George Meikle Kemp's death in 1844, his brother-in-law William Bonnar supervised its completion. Kemp's son Thomas placed the capstone.

The day was, however, marred by torrential rain and, according to an article in *The Renfrewshire Magazine* of 1846, the absence of the 'influential and elevated body of gentlemen, by whom it was originated' which

> *...resulted from the Modern Athenian aristocrats, who originally started the monument fund, refusing to interfere in the proceedings, on account of the plebeian ingredients of which the auxiliary committee was composed.*

Perhaps the aristocracy felt that they had done enough and were unwilling to put their hands in their pockets yet again. At least the merchants, the article pointed out, had avoided a second 'National Disgrace' – the half-finished National Monument on Calton Hill. This monument had been a topic dear to George's heart; he wrote an essay on the subject, proposing a whisky tax to fund its completion and suggesting that heroic incidents from Scottish history could be used to adorn it, much as those from Athenian history adorned the Parthenon. In 1842 he had drawn a proposed completion of it; the original of this drawing is held by the Scottish National Gallery, and it was engraved at least twice, in different versions, by Nichol and by West between 1842 and 1843.

It was some time before the Scott Monument took its present-day appearance. Only eight of the 64 sculptures planned for niches (of characters from Sir Walter Scott's novels and a few historical notables) were ready in time for the completion of the monument itself in 1844. Information on all the figures and their sculptors (one of whom was Amelia Paton, wife of the photographer David Octavius Hill) can be seen in the Edinburgh Museums Scott Monument Virtual Tour[3]. James Ballantine was a prime mover in obtaining the necessary funds for their completion and the remaining figures were made and placed in position in the years after 1871, the centenary of Scott's birth. The Centenary Dinner was the occasion of tributes to George by his friends, including David Cousin who was by then City Superintendent of Works for Edinburgh. The museum room on the first floor was fitted up by him, George having previously agreed to the suggestion by William Lindores that it would be a worthwhile addition to the monument (*The Scotsman*, 1 July 1840), although originally he had designed the second stage to be open. This room was completed in 1878, and in 1879 it became home to a collection of Scott memorabilia. Most of these items have been dispersed but in 2010 it was refurbished with display cabinets on the life of Sir Walter and visitor sound points, to add to the heraldic stained glass windows and wall carvings.

Maps from 1840 and 1850[4] show the monument as adjacent to Cleghorn's Nursery and Flower Gardens, whereas by 1860 the monument had been incorporated into East Princes Street Gardens, which by then

3 www.edinburghmuseums.org.uk/venues/scott-monument
4 www.edinphoto.org.uk

covered the nursery area. The gardens were a subject of controversy, as the area was being eyed up by greengrocers as a prime spot for market booths; Edinburgh City Council considered the area for a 'green' market in 1844. It is ironic that, this early scheme having failed in the 19th century, the area is now surrounded by booths during the annual Christmas market. One of the more inventive ideas for 'improving' the monument was a suggestion in a letter to *The Scotsman*, 30 December 1863, to furnish it with an electric clock with four dials, making use of the wire controlling the one o'clock gun. This idea was rightly dismissed as absurd in a follow-up letter and it was not carried out – although a large floral clock (dating from 1903 and the oldest in the world) was later placed further west in the gardens.

Opinion on the monument in the 19th century was generally very favourable, not only because of its intrinsic beauty and originality, but under the halo of its association with Sir Walter Scott. At a public meeting concerned with the monument held in 1844, the writer and critic Professor John Wilson of Edinburgh University said:

> *No doubt [Scott's] statue will there be gazed at reverentially – blessed in the murmuring voice of deep emotion – causing often the tear to start not only on the fair, but on the manly cheek.*

There were, however, dissenters: Lord Meadowbank described the monument as an 'abomination' and 'bastard gothic'. The art critic John Ruskin likened it to a candlesnuffer. He offered his own concept for a memorial: a colossal figure of Sir Walter placed in Salisbury Crags, with Borders shepherds reclining at his feet. He presented this idea in *The Architectural Magazine*, January 1839, in an essay on monumental sculpture and its proper location. Ruskin suggested that a city location, with its bustling crowds, can result in the aesthetics of the monument taking precedence over the feelings it was meant to engender. As it has turned out, the monument's location and unique design have given it an impact divorced from its original purpose – just as Ruskin had predicted.

What was the architectural originality of the Scott monument? George gathered varied elements from historic buildings to create the original idea of a massive Gothic spire, incorporating within it a canopied statue as a memorial. This was an innovation, as historically the monument would have been placed on the top rather than inside. Gifford *et al* in *The Buildings of Scotland: Edinburgh* noted its debt to previous buildings (Melrose Abbey, Glasgow, Rheims and Antwerp Cathedrals) but pointed out the following:

> *The great Gothic shrine was not an uncommon theme in the early 19C in the minds and drawings (at least) of visionary architects such as Schinkel. ...Kemp's achievement was to realise this romantic idea in archaeologically correct detail.*

The Scott Monument set a fashion, its most celebrated successor being Gilbert Scott's Albert Memorial in London. Here the arguments about the obelisk versus the Gothic cross for such memorials (which had been rehearsed in relation to the Scott Monument) arose once more. The success of the Scott Monument perhaps swayed opinion and Queen Victoria herself noted the resemblance of the Albert Memorial to the Scott Monument. The earlier Albert Memorial in Manchester designed in 1862 by Thomas Worthington (shown in Figure 41) bears an even closer resemblance to the Scott Monument. In Scotland similar examples are the Market Cross in Forres on the Moray coast (Thomas Mackenzie, 1844) and the Kenneth Murray Monument in Tain, Ross and Cromarty (Laurence Beveridge, 1879); Dunedin, New Zealand has the Cargill Monument (Charles Swyer, 1863-4).

While many neo-Gothic monuments may have owed something to the Scott Monument once it had been built and had become well known, George himself had little obvious influence on the architectural profession in his lifetime. One exception might be that he provided a catalyst to the arguments about who could or could not consider themselves as belonging to the profession, as Charles McKean has pointed out in *Scottish Architects' Papers*. Unlike established architects such as William Burn, George had no practice with junior architects that he

41 Manchester's Albert Memorial, Albert Square. Following an architectural competition, it was completed in 1866 by Alfred Waterhouse and was the first of several memorials to Prince Albert. It has been said to owe something to the Scott Monument, and may itself have influenced Gilbert Scott's Albert Memorial in London.

could train. Nevertheless, it was common for architects to hold informal lessons for the masons and other artisans working on site, as a contemporary architect James Gowans has described. James Gowans was similar to George in some ways, in that he was from a humble background, liked to sketch the Borders Abbeys, and created an extraordinary building, Rock Villa; unlike George he lived and worked to old age and was eventually knighted. Duncan McAra's biography quotes him, referring to his youth, as saying that

> *...there was at every important building a drawing class, usually conducted by the chief foreman or clerk of works.*

Indeed, George learned his craft on the job in this way while working for William Burn, and it is very likely that he would have performed this training role in his turn. He may well have set some of his humble craftsmen *en route* to their careers. One of them, George Lang (or Laing) was to become a leading builder in Canada, responsible for a large number of public buildings in Halifax, Nova Scotia.

Setting aside its influence on architecture, the Scott Monument has been the inspiration for a huge number of objects. Very intricate models were made with various materials, made possible in the 19th century by the invention by Benjamin Cheverton of the 'reducing machine'; this was a kind of three-dimensional pantograph, popularised by its presentation at the Great Exhibition of 1851. Items inspired by the monument include what might be called tourist tat – shortbread tins and the like – and advertising material, as well as items of artistic merit. Some examples of the wide range of articles inspired by the monument are shown in Figures 42-45. These ever-proliferating images have

42 Skeleton clock produced by William Frederick Evans of Handsworth and shown at the Great Exhibition of 1851. An example of the very intricate models made of the Scott Monument in the 19th century.

43 Chip-fork sculpture of the Scott Monument from the 2008 Edinburgh Festival Fringe, now held in the Museum Collections Centre, Edinburgh.

44 Tennent's Brewery lager label from the 2nd 'Scottish Series', an example of the use of the Scott Monument in advertising.

45 Brooch made by Hannah Louise Lamb, an example of the image of the Scott Monument used in a piece of modern jewellery.

turned the monument into an icon of the city and even of Scotland generally. Indeed, silver cruets in the shape of the monument have been used as symbols of Edinburgh at civic banquets. It has even featured in films (as a location in *Cloud Atlas*, released in 2012, and as a computer-generated image in *Death Defying Acts*, released in 2007).

Turning now to the current state of the monument itself, one can see the enormous problems that the choice of Binny sandstone created. The shale oil in the stone has leached out and mixed with smoke, especially from the railway, giving the monument its current black appearance. In the early 1990s, the City of Edinburgh Council performed a photogrammetric survey (in which very detailed survey drawings were produced from stereo photography), and restoration and cleaning commenced thereafter with funding from the Heritage Lottery Fund, Historic Scotland and the City of Edinburgh. Sadly, although £2.3 million has been spent, cleaning had to be abandoned because it might have led to the more intricate carvings being weakened and the risk of further weathering. The Edinburgh Museums Scott Monument Virtual Tour mentioned above gives more details of the process. In the basement of the monument there are kept supplies of recently quarried stone, available for repairs. Such repairs are bound to stand out against the oily blackness of the main structure and can give a kind of piebald effect in places (see Figure 46).

46 Repair of a sculpture of a dog on the Scott Monument, using recently quarried stone. The piebald effect is due to the contrast between the modern clean stone and the original stone, now blackened by soot combining with shale oil. Cleaning was stopped in the 1990s because of concerns about the fragility of the stone.

Today citizens of Edinburgh and tourists from all over the world almost universally admire the monument, and it is one of the most photographed sites in Edinburgh. Visitor numbers in recent years are typically 35-45,000 per year, although it is interesting to note that in the last years of the 1870s almost as many people visited: over 30,000 people according to *The Scotsman*, 12 July 1878. Those who climb the monument and make it to the fourth and topmost stage usually judge the effort worth the claustrophobic and vertigo-inducing 287 steps, and they receive a certificate. Those who cannot get to the top can rest in the museum room at the first stage where the stained glass windows can be admired; they will get an idea of the exhilarating view at the top from

47 The Scott Monument with Edinburgh Castle in the background to the left and Princes Street to the right. The St James Centre and Waverley Station are in the foreground.

many online contributions. The monument featured in the top 100 of Scotland's 'treasured places' as chosen by The Royal Commission on the Ancient and Historical Monuments of Scotland, whose very detailed information and images relating to the monument may be viewed online[5]. Figure 47 shows a classic view of the monument, towering above Princes Street and forming a centrepiece to Edinburgh itself.

5 www.canmore.rcahms.gov.uk

Chapter 8
Afterword: Who was George Meikle Kemp?

George Meikle Kemp was born in 1795 into a poor shepherding family near Biggar, Lanarkshire, in southern Scotland. After leaving school aged 14 he took up an apprenticeship in joinery before setting out by foot to travel around Scotland, England and the Continent. During these travels, he lived from hand-to-mouth, and studied and drew Gothic buildings. After setbacks in both his trade of joinery and in his self-chosen profession of architecture, he won, under a pseudonym, the competition to design the Scott Monument in Edinburgh. He supervised its construction – the largest monument to a literary figure in the world – but drowned in 1844 just before its completion, in somewhat mysterious circumstances.

George Meikle Kemp had a strange and rather contradictory personality. He was shy almost to the point of disability. Some of his social interactions (for example his anxiety about shaking hands with people) combined with his single-mindedness and ability to memorise precise details of buildings suggest that he was 'high on the autistic spectrum' as some psychiatrists would put it. Indeed Charles McKean noted in his essay in *Scottish Architects' Papers* that some contemporaries regarded him as 'no more than a mad carpenter'. He had a somewhat eccentric attitude to his own appearance, as indicated by stories about him 'unpolishing' his shoes when leaving his apprenticeship, and appearing at a committee with two collars on at the same time. The bouffant hairstyle he adopted and the wooden hat he made for himself were also a little unusual. He was observant of the social mores of others and keenly aware of his own background and place in society, and he was a patriotic Scotsman. However, judging by his letters, he was relatively uninterested in broader social issues. Despite his unusual and in some ways difficult personality, he made close and long-lasting friendships, and he married and had a family. His literary interests were remarkably wide for someone who left school at fourteen – his letters and poetry are full of classical and literary allusions – and he played the violin. Summing him up, it is difficult to better Robert Crawford who aptly described him in his book *On Glasgow and*

Edinburgh as a 'shy, bushy-haired, poetry-quoting joiner with a passion for Gothic architecture'.

His celebrity was fossilised and transmitted to our own time, partly through the tributes of his friends and family who were still active in public life at the time of his death aged 48, as well as through his spectacularly successful creation, the Scott Monument. It has led to a number of claims of kinship with him, and attributions of building and artworks, which are difficult to verify. The mystery is why he left little other than the monument except for a few, admittedly impressive, examples of joinery and architectural drawing. While he has been described as a watercolourist, there are few examples of this output to see (perhaps only one, that of the Royal Institution). His drawings are almost entirely in pen and ink or pencil. Most of his non-monument activities in the last decade of his life (the Scottish antiquities book, the Glasgow Cathedral reconstruction design, the Sueno's Stone idea, the North Bridge widening project) failed to materialise for various reasons, not all his fault. This biography, supported by recent scholarship, suggests that some of the buildings attributed to him are in fact by others. Indeed, there is no extant, complete building other than the Scott Monument that can be confidently attributed to him.

His intellectual abilities and drive are beyond doubt. A contemporary Edinburgh Town Councillor described him in 1842 as 'perhaps one of the cleverest men in the country as well as one of the most modest'. Samuel Smiles used him as a case study for his famous book *Self Help*. Many commentators have described him as a genius. Would he have been capable of even more stunning creations than the Scott Monument, had the opportunity arisen? He was probably not fully accepted by the architectural profession. His rival in the competition, David Roberts, resented his success and his previous employer, William Burn, was distrustful of his ability to stick to a brief. Despite his celebrity among the public, he was without obvious prospects for a regular income, and he was not part of a network of contacts. He was certainly not attuned to self-promotion or commercial activities and may even have had problems with drink, as a number of contemporaries have suggested. It is likely that the opportunities for fulfilling his talent were scarce and those that did appear (for example the wing at Woodhouselee) were inadequate to the scope of his vivid imagination, apparent in the letter in which he envisaged a heavenly figure and a gigantic horological apparatus covering the sky. It is possible that these visions were inflamed by alcohol or drugs but more probably they were a fundamental feature of his mind-set; he may have been indulging such visions during the long silences for which he was well known. His imagination needed for its successful outlet the impetus of a new large-scale project. This, sadly for him – and for us – was not available. The Scott Monument is the singular creation of a singular man. Its size, location and originality have made it an icon of Edinburgh and indeed of Scotland: a proud achievement for a self-taught shepherd's son.

Appendix
Sources of Material Relating to George Meikle Kemp

Likenesses

Likenesses of George Meikle Kemp include one (and possibly both) of those shown in Figure 33 (see page 83), and the portrait by Bonnar shown in Figure 35 (see page 87). The portrait of George holding the Scott Monument, shown on the back cover of this book, is stored in the Edinburgh City Art Centre, catalogued as 'by an unknown artist', although it would seem to be the image Bonnar described as being by David Hunter (also mentioned in correspondence of Mrs Kemp-Westren). A copy is on display in the museum room on the first floor of the Scott Monument. A bust by Alexander Handyside Ritchie is currently undergoing restoration in the Edinburgh Museum Collections Centre and is shown on the front cover of this book. The catalogue of the Scott Centenary Exhibition of 1871, where the bust was displayed, described it as the work of Ritchie and carved in marble by John Hutchison. There is a medallion portrait by Ritchie on the Kemp gravestone at St Cuthbert's Church. There are three photographs by Adamson and Hill, one of which can be seen in Figure 30 (see page 78).

Biographies

Thomas Bonnar wrote a life of George Meikle Kemp, his uncle by marriage, in the 1890s, some 50 years after Kemp's death. He used material from interviews with his aunt (Kemp's widow) and one of Kemp's friends, Alexander Keith, and he had access to family material such as letters and reminiscences. The antiquarian D.W. Kemp, carried out further research around the turn of the 20th century and started a second biography, the first few chapters of which are held in the National Archives of Scotland, along with the material he collected. John Faichney Methven wrote a short biography in 1988. N. M. McQ. Holmes and L. M. Stubbs gave an account of the history of the Scott Monument in 1979 which includes a short life of Kemp. There are entries on George Meikle Kemp in A *Biographical Dictionary of Eminent Scotsmen* (Chambers, 1855), *A Biographical Dictionary of British Architects 1600-1840* (Colvin, 1995), and by Charles McKean in the *Oxford Dictionary of National Biography* (2004).

Sources of documentary material

The most extensive collection of source material is the Kemp archive held at the Writers' Museum in Edinburgh. This contains original letters and texts, drawings and a few photographs and objects. It has been catalogued as far as possible with collection numbers and brief descriptions; a summary of its contents is given in Rebecca Bailey's *Scottish Architects' Papers*. It contains items relating to the Kemp family, including his sons Thomas and William, as well as to George Meikle Kemp himself. Other sources include the diaries of John Smith of Darnick, National Library of Scotland MS 8499 and 8499A; the Duke of Buccleuch's papers, National Archives of Scotland, NAS GD224/1071; records of Blackie and Son Ltd, University of Glasgow Archive Services, GB0248 and UGD61/2/1/1/1; contemporary newspaper articles, Post Office Directories and Parliamentary Reports; the EdinPhoto website; Biggar Museum Trust.

Drawings by George Meikle Kemp

The Scottish National Galleries hold the following drawings:

The Royal Institution, Edinburgh, D 4264 (see also *The Royal Institution*, William Deeble after George Meikle Kemp, P 3097, published 1839);

The West Bow, Edinburgh (with William Bonnar), D 2443;

View of the West Bow, Edinburgh (with William Bonnar), D 2444;

View of Heriot's Hospital and the Grassmarket from the Foot of the West Bow, Edinburgh, (with William Bonnar), D 2428 (date made 1850?);

The West Bow, Edinburgh (with William Bonnar), D 2444;

Calton Hill and surrounding scenery from Salisbury Crags, Edinburgh, with the National Monument as it would appear if completed, D 3801;

James Moir, PG1359 (unsigned; attributed to George Meikle Kemp).

The Central Library, Edinburgh, holds design sketches for the Scott Monument in a variety of media, and the following engravings:

The Royal Institution, Edinburgh, engr. W. Deeble (1837); Calton Hill, engr. James Johnstone;

Calton Hill and surrounding scenery from Salisbury Crags, with the National Monument as it would appear if completed, engr. J. West (1843);

Calton Hill (with proposed National monument) from the summit of Salisbury Crags, engr. Nichol (1843);

Edinburgh from the neighbourhood of Arthur Seat, engr. T. Dick (1829);

National Monument, Calton Hill, Edinburgh, engr. T. Dick;

St Giles Church, Edinburgh, engr. T. Dick;

Scott Monument, engr. Brown and Somerville (1840).

The Central Library, Edinburgh also holds a set of three notebooks, attributed to George Meikle Kemp; at least some of the material in the notebooks may be by his sons, according to a note by Howard Colvin. The City Art Centre, Edinburgh, also holds design sketches for the Scott Monument.

The Royal Commission on the Ancient and Historical Monuments of Scotland holds a few design drawings of the Scott Monument and of ecclesiastical buildings, including Melrose Abbey. Their online system CANMORE can be searched for the very extensive collection of photographs and other material relating to the Scott Monument.

Bibliography

Baile de Laperriere, C. (Ed) (1991) *The Royal Scottish Academy Exhibitors 1826-1990*, Hilmartin Manor Press, Calne, Wiltshire.

Bailey, R. M. (1996) *Scottish Architects' Papers: A Source Book*, Rutland Press, Edinburgh.

Bell, A. (Ed) (2005) *Lord Cockburn: Selected Letters*, John Donald, Edinburgh.

Billings R. W. (1845-52) *The Baronial and Ecclesiastical Antiquities of Scotland*, Blackwood and Sons, Edinburgh.

Bonnar, T. (1892) *Biographical Sketch of George Meikle Kemp: Architect of the Scott Monument*, Blackwood and Sons, Edinburgh.

Britton, J. (1814-1831) *Cathedral Antiquities*, Longman, London.

Cameron, D. K. (2006) *The Ballad and the Plough: Portrait of the Life of the Old Scottish Farmtouns*, Birlinn, Edinburgh.

Chambers, R. (1855) *A Biographical Dictionary of Eminent Scotsmen (Vol 5)*, Blackie and Son, Glasgow.

Christison, J. (1835) The Parish of Biggar (In: *The New Statistical Account of Scotland, Volume 7*), Blackwood and Sons, Edinburgh.

Colvin, H. M. (1995) *A Biographical Dictionary of British Architects 1600-1840*, 3rd Ed, Yale University Press, New Haven and London.

Crawford, R. (2013) *On Glasgow and Edinburgh*, Belknap Press of Harvard University Press, Cambridge, Mass.

Edinburgh (1972) *Catalogue of the Exhibition held at Edinburgh, in July and August 1871, on occasion of the commemoration of the centenary of the birth of Sir Walter Scott*, Constable, Edinburgh

Finley, G. (1980) *Landscapes of Memory: Turner as Illustrator to Scott*, University of California Press, Berkeley.

Gifford, J., McWilliam, C. and Walker, D. (1991) *The Buildings of Scotland: Edinburgh*, Penguin Books, London.

Halsby, J. and Harris, P. (2010) *The Dictionary of Scottish Painters 1600 to the Present*, Birlinn, Edinburgh.

Hitchin-Kemp, F. (1902) *A General History of the Kemp and Kempe Families of Great Britain and her Colonies*, Leadenhall Press, London.

Hogg, J. (1819) Storms, *The Blackwood's Magazine*, 5, 210-16.

Holmes, N. M. McQ. and Stubbs, L. M. (1979) *The Scott Monument: a History and Architectural Guide*, City of Edinburgh Museums and Art Galleries, Edinburgh.

Hughes, G. (1990) James Hogg and the Forum. *Studies in Hogg and his World*, 57-70.

Hunter, W. (1867) *Biggar and the House of Fleming*, Paterson, Edinburgh.

Kaufman, M. H. (2003) *The Regius Chair of Military Surgery in the University of Edinburgh, 1806-55*, Rodopi, Amsterdam, New York.

Kelly, S. (2002) *Scott-land: The Man Who Invented a Nation*, Birlinn, Edinburgh.

Lamont, S. (2001) *When Scotland Ruled the World: The Story of the Golden Age of Genius, Creativity and Exploration*, HarperCollins, London.

Lieuallen, R. (2002) *A Sculptor for Scotland: the Life and Work of Sir John Robert Steell, RSA (1804-1892)*, PhD thesis, University of Edinburgh.

McAra, D. (1975) *Sir James Gowans: Romantic Rationalist*, Paul Harris Publishing, Edinburgh.

Macaulay, J. (1997) The Demolition of the Western Towers of Glasgow Cathedral, in *The Architecture of Scottish Cities*, Ed: D. Mays.

McKean, C. and Walker, D. M. (1996) A Professorial on the Professional: A History of the Scottish Architectural Profession, in *Scottish Architects' Papers*, R. M. Bailey.

McKean, C. (2004) Kemp, George Meikle (1795-1844), *Oxford Dictionary of National Biography*, Oxford University Press, Oxford.

McLellan, A. (1836) *Plans and Elevations of the Proposed Restoration and Additions to Glasgow Cathedral*, Maclure and MacDonald, Glasgow.

McLeod, P. (1840) *New National Songs*, George Croall, Edinburgh (The Glen Collection of Scottish Music, National Library of Scotland).

Maggi, A. (2002) Documents relating to Roslin Chapel: a recently discovered collection of papers by John Britton, *Architectural Heritage, XIII*, 73-98.

Mays, D. (Ed) (1997) *The Architecture of Scottish Cities*, Tuckwell Press, East Linton.

Methven, J. F. (1988) *An Appreciation of the Life and Work of George Meikle Kemp Joiner and Architect*, The Methven Family Trust, Glasgow.

Miller, H. (1872) (Ed: J. Davidson) *Leading Articles on Various Subjects*, W. P. Nimmo, Edinburgh.

Nicholson, P. (1842) *Nicholson's New Carpenter's Guide*, G. Virtue, New York and London.

Robertson, D. (1842) *Whistle-binkie or the Piper of the Party; a Collection of Songs for the Social Circle, 4th series*, David Robertson, Glasgow.

Smiles, S. (2002) *Self-help; with Illustrations of Character, Conduct and Perseverance*, Oxford World's Classics, Oxford University Press, Oxford.

Stevenson, S. (1981) *David Octavius Hill and Robert Adamson: Catalogue of their Calotypes taken between 1843 and 1847 in the Collection of the Scottish National Portrait Gallery*, National Galleries of Scotland, Edinburgh.

Whitelaw, A. (1833) *The Republic of Letters, Vol IV*, Blackie and Sons, Glasgow.

Wylie, J. A. (1960) *Ter-centenary of the Scottish Reformation, as Commemorated at Edinburgh, August 1860*, John Maclaren, Edinburgh.

Picture Credits

1 © Crown Copyright/database right 2012, an Ordnance Survey/EDINA supplied service
2 From Bonnar (1892) *George Meikle Kemp*
3 Photo: P. L. Main
4 By permission of Glasgow Libraries
5 From Bonnar (1892) *George Meikle Kemp*
6 Courtesy of Robin Houston
7 © The Trustees of the British Museum, 1871, 0812.2754
8 © The Trustees of the British Museum, 1878, 0713.2028
9 Photo: P.L. Main
10 Courtesy of HathiTrust, www.hathitrust.org, record 011202884
11 © The Trustees of the British Museum, 1891, 0414.347
12 Photo: P. L. Main
13 © Scottish National Gallery, NG 2542
14 © The British Library Board, C.58.g.15 volume II, opposite 48
15 © The Trustees of the British Museum, 1888, 0612.874
16 Courtesy of Edinburgh Museums and Galleries
17 (a) Photo: M. J. Leese
(b) Courtesy of Georgian Antiques, www.georgianantiques.net
18 From Whitelaw (1833) *The Republic of Letters*
19 © The Trustees of the British Museum, 1864, 0309.223
20 Courtesy of Birlinn Ltd, www.birlinn.co.uk
21 Courtesy of the Maybole Home Page, www.maybole.org
22 © The Trustees of the British Museum, 1871,0812.1728
23 © RCAHMS, Licensor www.scran.ac.uk
24 © National Galleries of Scotland, Licensor www.scran.ac.uk
25 © City of Edinburgh Council, Licensor www.scran.ac.uk
26 © The City of Edinburgh Council, Licensor www.scran.ac.uk
27 Edinburgh City Libraries and Capital Collections, www.capitalcollections.org.uk

28 Photo: P. L. Main
29 Edinburgh City Libraries and Capital Collections, www.capitalcollections.org.uk
30 Edinburgh City Libraries and Capital Collections, www.capitalcollections.org.uk
31 Edinburgh City Libraries and Capital Collections, www.capitalcollections.org.uk
32 © Scottish National Gallery, D 4264
33 (a) From Bonnar (1892) *George Meikle Kemp*
(b) © Scottish National Portrait Gallery, PG 1359
34 From Bonnar (1892) *George Meikle Kemp*
35 © Scottish National Portrait Gallery, PG 246
36 Courtesy of the University of Toronto Libraries
37 Edinburgh City Libraries and Capital Collections, www.capitalcollections.org.uk, photo: F. M. Chrystal
38 Photo: P. L. Main
39 Courtesy of Edinburgh Museums and Galleries
40 Edinburgh City Libraries and Capital Collections, www.capitalcollections.org.uk
41 © David Dixon
42 Courtesy of Ian Burton Antique Clocks, www.ianburton.com
43 Courtesy of Edinburgh Museums and Galleries
44 Courtesy of Tennent's Brewery
45 Courtesy of Hannah Lamb, www.itchyfingers.org
46 Photo: Sandy Cowan
47 Scottish Viewpoint Picture Library, www.scottishviewpoint.com, photo: P. Tomkins

Bold page numbers refer to figures

Index

A

Adamson, Robert. *See* photography, early
Albert Memorial, London 102
Albert Memorial, Manchester 102, **103**
Amiens Cathedral 42
Anderson's Institution, Glasgow 21, 39
Antwerp Cathedral 42, **43**, 102
Apprentice Pillar. *See* Rosslyn Chapel
architectural profession 21, 30, 31, **32**, 57, 86, 91, 102, 111

B

Ballantine, James 73, 86, 100
Ballingall's Museum of Military Surgery 50
Beauvais Cathedral 42
Biggar **14**, 15, 18, 20, 27, 110
Billings, Robert William 29, 81
Binny sandstone **70**, 105, 106
Blackadder, Dame Elizabeth 98
Blackie and Son 54, 80
Blore, Edward 57
Board of Manufactures' Drawing Academy 84
Bonnar
  Elizabeth 52, 54. *See also* Kemp, Elizabeth, GMK's wife
  John 93
  Thomas 11, 14, 15, 16, 40, 45, 48, 52, 67, 82, **87**, 114
  William, GMK's brother-in-law **17**, **53**, 82, 83, 86, **87**, 92
  William, GMK's father-in-law 52
Bowhill House 51
Braidwood family 17, 18, 96
Britton, John 54, 68, 86
Buccleuch, Duke of 51, 52, 63, 97
Burns, Robert 18, **28**, 71
Burn, William 51, 67, 81, 86, 103, 111

C

Cadell, Robert 65
Caledonian Railway Company 70
Canterbury Cathedral 40
Cargill Monument, Dunedin 102
Carlyle, Thomas 33
Carnwath **14**, 19
Chantrey, Francis 71, 84
Cheverton, Benjamin 104
Classical style, in 19thC architecture **39**, **63**, 65, **82**
Cloud Atlas 105
Cockburn, Lord 92
Collie, James 55
Colvin, Howard 12, 46, 116
Cousin
  David 37, 48, 57, 59, 62, 100
  John 37, 52
Crossraguel Abbey 59

D

Da Vinci Code, The 29
Dalkeith 51, 52, 97
Death Defying Acts 105
debating societies 89
Demarco, Richard 68
Dick-Lauder, Sir Thomas 93
Dingwall 16
Donaldson's Hospital, Edinburgh 96
Drummond, James 52
Dryburgh Abbey 37, 62

E

Ebsworth, Joseph Woodfall 68, **69**
Edinburgh
  Calton Hill **60**, 80

Central Library 115
City Museums 75, 100, 106, 114
National Monument 99
New Town 38, **69**
North Bridge 68, **69**, 111
Princes Street 10, **39**, 59, **60**, 68, **69**, 100, 107
Salisbury Crags 80, 101
St Cuthbert's Church 54, 69, 94, **94**, 114
St Giles' Cathedral 73, 80, **80**
Stockbridge 54, 83
Union Canal 70, 90, 91, **91**
Writers' Museum 37, 49, 59, 62, 75, 79, 97, 115
Edinburgh Tee-total Band 73
educational system, Scottish 26
Elsrickle 25, 26
Ettrick Shepherd. *See* Hogg, James

F

Finley, Gerald 65
Forres 89
Forrest, Sir James 73
Freemasons 10, 48, 49, 73, 97, 98

G

Galashiels 36
Glasgow 39
Cathedral 53, 54, **56**, 58, 59, 68, 79, 81, 102, 111
Gallowgate 20, **21**
McLellan Galleries 55
St Mary's Episcopal Church 62
Gothic style, in 19thC architecture 11, 63, **64**, 65, **66**, 67, 101, 102, **103**
Gowans, Sir James 103
Graham, James Gillespie 55
Great Exhibition 104
Grieve, James 30

H

Halifax, Nova Scotia 103
Halkett, Craigie 98
Hamilton, Thomas 50, 65
Harvey, George 52
Heritage Lottery Fund 105
Hill, David Octavius. *See* photography, early
Hillridge. *See* Hillriggs
Hillriggs **14**, 18, **19**
Historic Scotland 58, 90, 105
Hogg, James 45, 89
Houston, Robin 15, 19
Hughes, Gillian 89
Hunter, David 114
Hutchison, John 114

J

Jedburgh Abbey 37, 79
Jeffrey, Lord 73, 93
John Watson's Institution, Edinburgh 96
Johnstone, James 54, 79

K

Keith, Alexander 114
Kelly, Stuart 74
Kelso Abbey 79
Kemp families, unrelated 15, 16, 98
Kemp, D.W. 15, 16, 18, 19, 20, 114
Kemp, Elizabeth, GMK's daughter 84
Kemp, Elizabeth, GMK's wife 62, 67, **96**, 114.
Kemp, George Meikle
as architect 30, **43**, 50, **51**, 55, **56**, 57, 58, 59, 62, 65, **66**, 75, **78**, 85, 89, 102, 110
as artist 50, **51**, 54, 55, **56**, **66**, 79, **80**, 81, **82**, 83, 85
as woodworker 11, 30, 32, 46, 49, **49**, 55, 97, 110
controversies 42, **43**, 55, 64, 65, 81, 92, 93, 101

correspondence 28, **41**, 42, **44**, 46, 52, 53, 55, 65, 67, 79, 89, 93
death **91**, 110
early years **14**, 18, 19, 24, 26, 27, **28**, 41
education 17, 26, 30, 32, 38, 39, 46
finances 51, 75, 78, 79, 81, 84, 89, 90, 96, 111
friends 55, 59, 65, 68, 84, 88, 93, 110
homes 21, **24**, 36, 39, 40, 46, 54, 64, 84, 85, 93
likenesses **78**, **83**, 86, **87**, 114
memorials to 11, **30**, 36, 93, **94**
musical interests 33, 87, **88**
personality 12, 26, 31, 36, 40, 42, **44**, 50, 53, 54, 57, 68, 73, 88, 89, 90, 110, 111
poetry composition **24**, 31, 33, 41, 45, 49, 54, **88**, 110
proposed book by 79, **80**, 111
social attitudes **41**, 72, 89, 110
travels 36, 41, 46, 52, 84, 89, 110
working methods 37, 38, 53, 75, **78**, 90, 110
Kemp, James, GMK's father **14**, 15, 16, **17**, 24
Kemp, Jane, GMK's daughter 84, 96
Kemp, Thomas, GMK's brother 97
Kemp, Thomas, GMK's son 37, 54, 84, **85**, 97, **99**
Kemp, Violet, GMK's sister 11, 14, **27**, 45, 98
Kemp, William, GMK's son 84
Kemp-Westren, Elizabeth 97
Kenneth Murray Monument, Tain 102
Kilwinning Abbey 59

L

Laing, George. *See* Lang, George
Lambie, Brian 19
Lamont, Stewart 33
Lang, George 103
Learmonth, John 62
Leith 37, 42, 71
Leiver, A.W. 64
Libberton **14**, 15
Lieuallen, Rocco 71
Lind, David 69, 73, 90, 92
Lindores, William 100
Linlithgow Palace 64
London **41**, 62, 102
St Paul's Cathedral 40

M

Macaulay, James 57
Maggi, Angelo 86
Manchester 39, **103**
Market Cross, Forres 102
Maybole **30**, 58
McAra, Duncan 103
McKean, Charles 57, 102, 110
McLaggan, Alex 86
McLellan, Archibald 55, 79
McLeod, Peter 86
Meadowbank, Lord 65, 101
Meikle, George 20, **21**
Meikle, James 19
Melrose Abbey 36, 37, **38**, **51**, 58, 62, 79, 102
Methven, John Faichney 114
Millburn Church, Renton 58
Millburn Tower, Ratho 58
Miller, Hugh 10, 78, 91, 93, 96
Moir, James **83**
Moorfoot 14, 16, 18, **24**, 25
Morvo, John 37, 62, 64
Mossman, John 26
Mossman, William 26
Mowbray family 19, 25
Mowbray, Jean 14, 17, 25, 45
Mowbray, Joseph 79

N

Nasmyth, Alexander 38, **39**
National Galleries of Scotland 81, 82, 100, 115
National Portrait Gallery, London 98

Newhall **14**, 18, 25, 28, 54
Nicholson, Peter 31, **32**
Ninemileburn 27
Noble, Andrew 30
Noble, James 31, 48, 59

O

Oxton 15

P

Paton, Amelia 100
Peebles **14**, **30**
Penicuik **14**, 18
Pentland Hills 14, **14**, 25
photography, early 68, **70**, **74**, **78**, 98, 114
Pitconie, Felice 42, **85**
Playfair, John 45
Playfair, William Henry **63**
Presbyterianism 20, 33, 41
Pugin, Augustus 57

R

Rae, Gilbert 17, 19, 25
Rae, William 73
Redscarhead 30
Rheims Cathedral 102
Rickman, Thomas 63, 64
Ritchie, Alexander Handyside 73, **94**, 114
Roberts, David 63, **64**, 73, 111
Rochead, John 58
Rosebery, Lord 18
Roslin Castle 28, 84
Roslin Inn 29
Rosslyn Chapel **29**, 58, 84, 85
Royal Commission on the Ancient and Historical Monuments of Scotland 107, 116
Royal Institute of British Architects 86
Royal Institution **39**, 81, **82**
Royal Scottish Academy 52, 63, 81, **82**, 94
Ruskin, John 101

S

Scotch Malt Whisky Society 11
Scots language 42, **88**, 92
Scott Centenary 31, 75, 100, 114
Scott Monument
  Act of Consent 75
  committees 62, 73, 98
  competition 10, 37, 62, **63**, **64**, **66**, 73, 80
  construction **70**, **74**, **78**, 100, 110
  deterioration of stone **70**, 105, **106**
  financing of 57, 62, 68, 98, 100
  foundation 10, 73
  inauguration ceremony 98, **99**
  influence on other works 102, **103**, **104**, **105**
  museum room 73, 100, 106, 114
  present day 68, 100, 105, **107**
  sculptures **72**, 100, **106**
  site 38, 62, 69, 101
  statue of Sir Walter Scott 71, **72**
  surroundings 98, 100
  time capsule 10, 73
Scott, Gilbert 102
Scott, Robert 21, 62
Scott, Sir Walter 10, 18, 30, **36**, 52, 62, 65, **72**, 74, 85, 101
Scottish Academy. *See* Royal Scottish Academy
Self Help. *See* Smiles, Samuel
shepherding 14, 16, **17**, 18, 25, 27, 71, 101
Smiles, Samuel 11, 111
Smith, John, of Darnick 52
St Geneviève, Church of, Paris 42
St Vulfran, Church of, Abbeville 42
Steell, Sir John 71, 81
Stevenson, Sara 98
stonemasons 37, 48, **74**, 78, 93, 98
Sueno's Stone 89, 111

T

Tain 102
Telford, Thomas 33
Temple 15
The Witness. *See* Miller, Hugh
Thomson, Adam 26
Thomson, Robert Kemp **96**, 97
Trinity College Kirk 58
Turner, J.M.W. 65
Tytler, James 90

U

University of Edinburgh 50
University of Glasgow 80
University of Strathclyde 40

V

Victoria, Queen 71, 75, 102

W

Walker, David 57
Walston **14**, 17, 25, 26
West Linton **14**, 25
Whistle-binkie 86, **88**
Whitecastle 15
Wigtown 97
Wilson, John 101
Woodhouselee 90, 112
Worthington, Thomas 102

Y

York Minster 39

Colophon

Printed and bound in Great Britain by Berforts in Hastings, East Sussex, on 130gsm silk.

Book design, layout and typesetting by Omnis Partners, Cumbernauld, Scotland.

Typefaces; Versa, Versa Condensed and Versa Sans (Peter Verheul).